THE BANG STORY

From the Basement to the Bright Lights ...

FRANK GILCKEN - TONY DIORIO - FRANK FERRARA
with **LAWRENCE KNORR**

SUNBURY
P R E S S
Mechanicsburg, PA USA

Published by Sunbury Press, Inc.
Mechanicsburg, Pennsylvania

SUNBURY
P R E S S
www.sunburypress.com

For information about special discounts for bulk purchases, please
contact Sunbury Press Orders Dept. at (855) 338-8359 or orders@
sunburypress.com.

To request one of our authors for speaking engagements or book
signings, please contact Sunbury Press Publicity Dept. at publicity@
sunburypress.com.

ISBN: 978-1-62006-582-2 (Trade paperback)
ISBN: 978-1-62006-776-5 (Mobipocket)

Library of Congress Control Number: 2017951502

SECOND SUNBURY PRESS EDITION: January 2018

Product of the United States of America
0 1 1 2 3 5 8 13 21 34 55

Set in Bookman Old Style
Designed by Crystal Devine
Cover by Lawrence Knorr
Edited by Lawrence Knorr

Continue the Enlightenment!

DEDICATIONS

OUR PARENTS & FAMILY
Andrea & Carmela, Anthony & Teresa, Moe & Dottie.

From Tony:
To Jeanie and my kids: Kim, Michelle, and Anthony.
It was a special time in our lives. Thank you for
supporting my dream and sorry for all the loud BANGin'.

RICK & DONNA BOWEN
Rick, we found you in Orlando and you turned our dream
into reality.

TOMMY WINGATE
The best road manager ever. Your personality and sense of
humor made everything so much fun.

STEVE HINER
Your dedication and hard work were more than we could
have hoped for. I can still hear your voice and see your
smile. We miss you everyday.

DANNY SIMMONDS
Your friendship and the art you created for us was
amazing. We will always have a strong connection.

DON NAPLES
From building our PA system to taking care of our
recording needs, you were always there for us.

BRUCE GARY
Your incredible talent and creativity were instrumental in
creating our style. We miss you my friend.

TO ALL OUR FANS AROUND THE WORLD
Your love and support are priceless.

Contents

CHAPTER 1

Childhood Friends

WHEN FRANKIE GILCKEN first met Frank Ferrara in the first grade in 1959, Frankie recalled Frank as a 'little Italian kid who couldn't speak any English.' Gilcken, a self-described shy kid himself, took Ferrara under his wing and the two became fast friends.

Gilcken was born on July 10, 1953, in Chester, Pennsylvania, a suburb on the south side of Philadelphia, near the Navy Yard, Sun Oil refinery, and the airport. He was the son of Delbert "Moe" and Dottie Gilcken. Moe, a hard-working laborer at the Sun facility, died in 1968, when Frankie was only fourteen. Dottie was the prototypical housewife of that era, always supportive of her musically-talented son, even through the tough times of Frankie's fatherless teenage years.

"My two older sisters, Ellen and Lois, were my first musical influences," said Frankie. "They played records and danced all the time. I did Elvis Presley impersonations for them when I was only three. It was my sisters who turned me on to the 1950s music by Elvis and Ricky Nelson and others."

Dottie Gilcken took her son to shows at the Steel Pier, in Atlantic City, beginning when he was ten. Young Gilcken witnessed the Four Seasons, Ricky Nelson, and Herman's Hermits, all of which influenced his early musical taste.

"My uncle Joe Smith was a guitarist who played hillbilly music at the fire hall," said Gilcken. "He was a fireman. He gave me my first guitar when I was three. I used to hold it while singing 'Hound Dog.'"

It wasn't until he was eleven, though, that Frankie Gilcken received his first guitar lesson from Ricky Giordano, who worked at Caruso Brother's Music Store, after his father had bought him a guitar for $600 and his grandmother had purchased his first amplifier. Giordano and the Caruso Brothers were a musical institution in Chester, Pennsylvania. Gilcken was very fortunate to have such a highly-respected and influential teacher.

"Marty Caruso was the music director for *Al Albert's Showcase*, a variety show that aired on WKBS-TV (UHF Channel 48), a local television station," said Gilcken.

Gilcken and his friend, Joe Hooker, ended up on the show when he was twelve. They had joined a band called The Gems that also included the Ritz brothers, Mike, aged thirteen, and Larry, aged nine. Frankie joined this band after only one week of guitar lessons. Both he and Hooker played guitars, Mike was on drums and little Larry sang and played the tambourine. The four played "Hungry" by Paul Revere and the Raiders on the TV show. The peach-fuzzed quartet also landed a spot on Tony Grant's *Stars of Tomorrow* on the Steel Pier, in Atlantic City, where they played the Beatles' "Run for your Life."

"We were on the Steel Pier for a week," said Frankie. "It was the same week the Supremes were there, playing on the big stage. We got to watch them every day."

It was Mrs. Ritz, the mother of two of The Gems, who arranged the shows and television appearances. The young band played at a club called The Stardust, in Chester. The boys had to stay in the kitchen until they were to perform because they were many years under age. It was at the Stardust where the boys met the Comets, who were playing without Bill Haley, who was out of the country. Gilcken recalled Chester native Rudy Pompilli, the saxophone player and longest-tenured Comet, teaching him how to entertain the crowd.

"Rudy was a big influence on my development of stage presence," said Frankie. "He gave us kids pointers about how to move on stage."

FRANK FERRARA WOULD watch The Gems play at the Linwood Youth Center. The two had been separated for several years as they attended different schools. But now, at age thirteen, they were back together. One day, The Gems invited him to play bass for them. Frank went to the pawn shop to pick up a bass guitar. But, The Gems broke up soon after.

Francesco (Frank) Ferrara was born on the Ides of March (March 15), 1953, in the village of Monteforte Irpino in the Campania region of southern Italy, near Avellino, about thirty-five miles east of Naples. He was the son of Andrea and Carmela Ferrara.

In November 1954 Andrea journeyed to Pennsylvania to set up a new life for the family. He settled in the suburb of Linwood, Pennsylvania, on the south side of Philadelphia, just a few minutes from the Delaware line. A mostly Italian neighborhood, it was thriving at the time, thanks to the proximity to the Sun Oil refinery and airport.

Francesco was five years old when the family, including two older sisters, Gerardina and Giovanna, journeyed via the ship *S.S. Independence* from Naples, Italy, to Ellis Island. They arrived on June 13, 1958. Upon arrival, all but Carmela's name was changed. Andrea became Andrew. Gerardina became Gerri. Giovanna became Joann. And, Francesco became Francis—a name which Frank hated. Ultimately, he convinced everyone to call him Frank.

Andrew Ferrara was a laborer at a smelting company in Wilmington, Delaware. He also did odd jobs around the neighborhood—whatever work he could find. "My dad had a lot of energy for work," said Frank. "He was always doing something. I don't remember him ever sitting around." The senior Ferrara had been a POW during World War II. When Italy began to fall to the allies, the Germans rounded up all of the Italian soldiers and put them into internment camps.

"I remember the stories my father would tell me about the war," recalled Frank. "The soldiers were starving and the Germans would sometimes throw a horse tail in the cage and laugh as the Italians scrambled for it and fought over it. Until the war was over, my mom had no idea if he was alive. It is amazing he survived."

In Italy, the Ferraras lived in Francesco's grandfather's house, along with his uncle's family. Life was a struggle. Carmela's father, Martino Fusco, had left for the USA over twenty years prior after his wife died, leaving Carmela, at age 18, to care for her brothers and sisters.

Carmela Ferrara was a housewife known for her fabulous cooking, including her gnocchi, eggplant parmesan, and pasta fagiole (pronounced fa-zool). Only when the kids were a little older, did Carmela take a job outside the home, working in the kitchen at Frank's school.

"My dad made four barrels of wine each year," said the younger Ferrara, "and mom always made and bottled her sauce. They had a full garden in the backyard with basil and tomatoes. Dad dug out a full basement with a shovel and a bucket so they had a place to store their wine and tomato sauce. I still have his wine press. This later became the place where we practiced. Dad always shared his wine with others—would give my friends a nip. My dad loved to have fun and he deserved to because he worked all the time. I wish I had his energy and discipline."

Andrew realized his son was very different from himself, so he adjusted his expectations. While he was earning about $40 a week as a laborer, he bought Frank his first bass for $80.

Because Frank was the only boy in the family, he got what he wanted. His oldest sister, Gerri, and middle sister, Joann, assisted with the housework. Frank did not hang around the family. Music was his calling.

Frank recalled watching the Beatles on Ed Sullivan when he was 11 years old. John, Paul, George, and Ringo were definitely an inspiration. As he picked up the bass at age 14, he began playing with Frankie.

Purple Haze, named after the Jimi Hendrix tune, was the first band that Frank and Frankie played in after The Gems, when they were in there early teens. Frankie first taught the Beatles' "Honey Don't" to Frank on the bass. Frank never learned to read music and never took a lesson—Gilcken was his teacher. Next, they were playing "All Day and All of the Night" by the Kinks. Frank was a quick learner and the two really had a lot of fun. Besides being huge Beatles fans, they listened to Jimi Hendrix and went to Cream and Iron Butterfly concerts and played their songs in Purple Haze. Besides Frank and Frankie, Joe Hooker played the organ, George Emmertz the guitar, and Dennis Westman the drums. Joe and Frank were the singers. The band lasted about a year, until Joe Hooker left.

Around that time, the road managers for the Soul Survivors, Jay Felkoff and Paul Lichter, were looking for a band to back up the popular local singer, Karen Young. The boys got together with her and called themselves Sandd. They played around town a lot—at nightclubs and bars in Philadelphia. Frank and Frankie were 16 and were trying to go to school and play in the band. They were making money and doing what they loved to do, so they both dropped out of high school in 10th grade.

Sandd's big break came on January 17, 1969, when the Rascals played the Spectrum before a crowd of 10,000. Sweetwater was supposed to open the concert but were involved in an automobile accident. Promoters Lou Petro and Peter DePaul scrambled to find replacements, quickly settling on New Hope (formerly Kit Kat), Pazant Brothers, and Sandd. The latter was the opening band and played one set.

Karen Young, who later had a disco hit in the 70s, belted out the songs, while the boys played behind her, in front of thousands. At one point, Karen nearly met with catastrophe. She was on the floor with the crowd and tried to return to the stage by standing on a folding chair. This suddenly collapsed but she luckily fell back into the arms of manager Paul, who caught her.

"The crowd was really cool," recalled Frank, "but the coolest thing that day was when the limo for the Rascals arrived and Dino Danelli stepped out in a fur coat. He looked like a rock star!"

Sandd lasted nine months. Ferrara would drive around town and pick everyone up to practice in center city. They would buy song books and cut out the pages with the lyrics. But, one day, Karen Young and the drummer both quit. So, Frankie and Frank put an ad in the paper for a drummer. That's when Tony Diorio responded.

...

"Look beyond the stars
To your dreams that shine forever on
Look past the shadows
For they'll remain until your dead and gone

—Lyrics from *Little Boy Blue*

Ferrara Family

Arrived on the Independence to America
from Monteforte Irpino, Italy

Andrea Ferrara
Born 1912

Gerardina Ferrara
Born 1947

Giovanna Ferrara
Born 1951

Carmela Ferrara
Born 1915

Francisco Ferrara
Born 1953

Photo Editing: Eric J. Kraus.

Frank Ferrara passport photo.

Frank Ferrara school picture.

Frank Ferrara in high school.

The Gems appearing on the Tony Grant show in 1965.

Frank holding his first bass, 1967.

Frank's Mom and Pop in the backyard with Peppy.

Frankie Gilcken and his brother Bobby, 1967.

Frankie's mom, Dot, and father, Moe.

Sandd performing at the 19th Hole Lounge in Philadelphia, 1970.

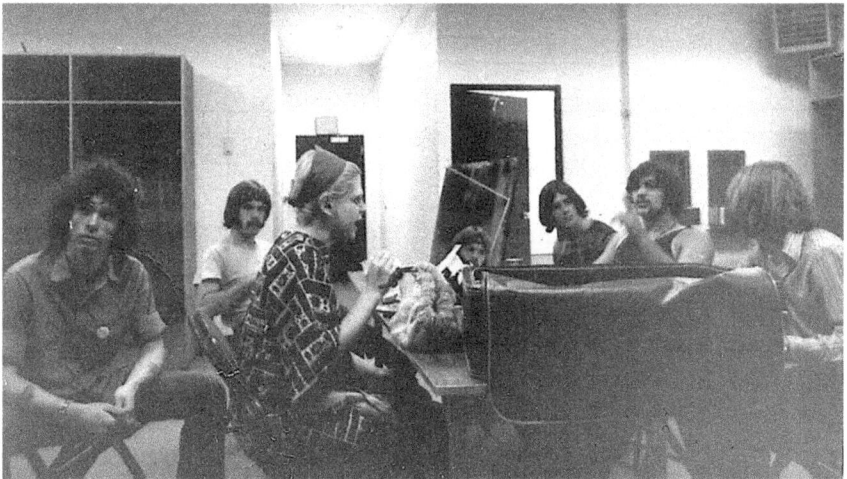

Sandd backstage before the Rascals show.

Magic Band

ANTHONY "TONY" DIORIO, a first generation Italian-American, was born in Wilmington, Delaware, July 9, 1943, the son of Anthony and Teresa Rose (Elia) Diorio, on the same day the Allies invaded Sicily.

"I had a good childhood," recalled Tony. "We were one of the first families on the block to have a TV, around 1948 or 1949. It had a little 8-inch screen and I sat on the back of a chair watching kids shows and rodeos. Later on, there was a TV show I loved called *Willy the Worm*, a puppet show produced in Philadelphia. I sent away for a *Willy the Worm* gas mask for a couple bucks and got back a genuine war surplus gas mask. These were the pioneer days of television."

Tony's great-great grandfather had come to America to work on the Transcontinental Railroad, in the 1860s but went back to Italy complaining, "Those people are not civilized!"

Half a century later, Tony's father came to America at age five, in 1916, eventually meeting Teresa Rose Elia of Poland, a small coal mining town in Pennsylvania. They married and settled in northern Delaware, close to many relatives in the surrounding region. Two daughters were born before their only son. The eldest daughter, Anita, died young from pneumonia, before penicillin. Tony grew up with his older sister Aline.

During the war, Anthony senior went to work at a war factory in Marcus Hook, PA. He was put in charge of inventory and his co-workers complained that he worked too hard. "My dad had an incredible work ethic," said Tony. "He never yelled or raised his hand to me. My mom once chased me around the table with a brush, that was the extent of any corporal punishment ever coming my way.

"My parents wanted to be fully American. They were a typical 1950s family, complete with the wood-paneled bar in the basement, with photos of all their friends on the walls and plenty of cocktail parties held there.

"My parents both came from big families and so I had lots of aunts and uncles and cousins around all my life. There were many family events so large that sometimes we'd rent a firehouse. Oh, and the food! It was the Italian way of life: family and eating.

"Before World War II, my dad had borrowed $500 to open a small store. As time went by, he grew his store into a chain of five and dime stores known as Richardson Variety Stores. My mom created hundreds of handmade Easter baskets every year, so popular people would come from miles away to buy them."

Tony grew up working in the store chain as a stock boy, before graduating to manager. Soon, he realized five and dimes were on the way out. The big boys of retail were moving in. Tony wanted to try a different business model, seeing that discounters were coming of age. He started buying closeouts and surplus wholesale, which caused an immediate impact on the bottom line. In his early twenties, he took over the business.

"One Christmas, I bought a bunch of closeouts of Mattel toys and ran a Peter Max-style ad campaign," recalled Tony. "I was doubling my money and the big boys were coming over to see how I was doing it. I bought 100,000 Hot Wheels, retailing everywhere for a dollar and sold them four for a dollar. I sold GI Joe dolls for $2, when they were normally going for $8. I made a killing. I was buying railroad box cars of paper towels from Scott's Paper because the print was bad and the product was not shrink-wrapped. I would get closeouts in Philly, New Jersey, and New York. I was riding high and having fun."

When Tony was younger, his father was a friend of the manager of the "godfather" of rock and roll, Bill Haley and the Comets. Haley lived a few miles away, in Aston, Pennsylvania. One day, the manager brought over a couple of albums. Tony played them for hours. "Get out in that kitchen and rattle those pots and pans," Bill Haley sang. Those songs were forever ingrained in Tony's brain.

"In December of 1963, I fell in love with rock and roll," recalled Tony. "I was driving my mom's car home one night, listening to the radio, when the DJ announced, 'I have a new group with a new sound from Liverpool, England—the Beatles.' He played 'I Wanna Hold Your Hand,' and I was hooked.

At the time, Tony was reading a lot of science fiction books and starting to write poetry and short stories. It was not until he was twenty-five, though, with a wife and three kids, that he began to play music. He picked up a guitar and keyboards but couldn't grasp it. Then, he looked at the drums and realized, "I can do that. You don't have to think about it, just feel the music and practice, practice, practice."

His first band was called December's Children. They played soul music, circa 1967 or 1968, covering songs from the Righteous Brothers and the Rolling Stones. "We practiced in an old burger joint after hours. We had a great soul singer but never went anywhere," recalled Tony. "The band wanted to play clubs full-time but this was not big enough for me to leave the retail business, so they went off to become professionals and I went back to selling white socks."

Tony then bounced around to different part-time groups, drumming for a soul band at the Bloody Bucket, in Rehoboth Beach, Delaware, then joined a band, The Four Trends, who dressed in blazers and ties, and played upscale private and frat parties. Tony recalled one in particular, "Once we played the DuPont estate in Beaver Valley, Delaware. This was a huge mansion and the crowd was the upper crust of Delaware elite. I still remember the game room loaded with heads of animals on the walls, standing stuffed bears and elephant tusks."

Tony continued practicing his drums, always working to improve. Said Tony, "I was practicing constantly in the basement of my house. I drove my family nuts for hours every day. I was so into it, once I bought a little mike mixer and put microphones in all my drums with an amp and speakers. At the same time, in another part of the basement, I had hundreds of gallons of fish tanks raising tropical fish for a pet store I had opened."

After hearing The Doors' "Light My Fire" at a party—all seven minutes of it—Tony recognized a shift in popular music. Then, the love and peace movement took hold. Tony began wearing beads and a Nehru jacket and soon dropped out of The Trends.

All the while, Tony was continuing to run five stores with sixty employees but the thrill was gone. He no longer had the passion to blaze new trails in retail. His heart was set on music.

IN MID-AUGUST 1969 sixteen year-old Frank Ferrara spray-painted his 1965 Mustang purple and loaded up with some friends to head to Woodstock. Frankie Gilcken was unable to join them, having had a severe reaction to some drugs at the Atlantic City Pop Festival, held two weeks prior. After returning from Woodstock, Frank and Frankie placed an advertisement in the *Philadelphia Inquirer* seeking a drummer.

"I saw an ad in the Philadelphia paper: looking for a drummer. I just had a feeling about it," recalled Tony.

Tony responded to the ad and soon had a meeting with Frankie Gilcken and Frank Ferrara. "We hit it off like magic," explained Tony. "They were sixteen and I was twenty-six with three kids. I was somewhat an executive type, with all of the trappings: a new 240Z, American Express card—the works. The Franks and I were soon practicing in Philly, auditioning front men and keyboard players, eventually moving to the basement of the Claymont, Delaware, store. The neighborhood kids would gather outside and listen to the band through the metal grates. We were loud!"

They immediately began writing their own music. Gilcken and Ferrara had been writing songs since they were 14—"Fade Away" being their first. Now Frankie Gilcken was taking jazz lessons and incorporating them into his writing, giving it a psychedelic sound with many changes of tempo.

Tony, who had been writing poetry since he was a child, was an avid reader of science fiction and always followed the news. He would write lyrics by coming up with a line or two and then going through the alphabet to find rhymes.

"The lyrics were the biggest thing about our songs," said Frank Ferrara, "and with *Death of a Country*, we always wrote depressing songs. But, after *Death of a Country*, everything was positive."

In those early days, the band rehearsed by playing the Beatles or Black Sabbath, quickly developing their own songwriting aspirations, with Diorio supplying the lyrics to the riffs and melodies of Gilcken and Ferrara. "A lot of the times, the way we'd write songs is that I'd write something and give it to the Franks and they'd make it into a song," explained Tony. "Or they'd have a riff and I'd come up with a lyric line and we'd go from there. I would write as they were playing. They put it to music, basically. Some of the songs, we'd have an idea and we'd just go with it musically and lyrically at the same time. Frank usually came up with the melody and Frankie usually came up with the riff—the hook of the song.

"Being major fans of the Beatles," continued Tony, "one day, early on, during a practice, we decided to try to call Paul McCartney, in England, to see if he could help our band get started. After finally finding the number of Abbey Road studios, we called. When a voice answered, we excitedly asked for Paul. The voice on the other end said he was 'the janitor cleaning up and it was the middle of the night and Mr. McCartney wasn't in and we should call back.' Still amazing the things you do to try and get your career started. They were working on *Let it Be*."

Not soon after, on April 10, 1970, Paul announced he was leaving the Beatles, culminating in their break-up. The band doubts the late-night phone call had any bearing on the decision.

"We practiced, we worked and we ate cheesesteaks from the Claymont steak shop. A good friend and neighbor, Don Naples, took care of our technical needs," continued Tony. "We first practiced in center city Philadelphia, in a second-story place. Ticketron was next door. We called ourselves the Magic Band."

Frank recalled, "Tony would pick us up and drive to Philly to rehearse. On this particular day, a Saturday, I was at Rockford Park, in Wilmington, hanging with some friends when someone asked me if I wanted to do acid. I had never done acid and did not know what to expect. After about fifteen or twenty minutes, I didn't feel any different. So I just figured the acid wasn't very good.

"Just about then, we were throwing a football around. I went long to catch a pass. As I turned around, the guy threw the ball. As soon as it left his hand, the acid kicked in and, all of a sudden, everything went into slow-motion. All I could see was a trail of the football coming my way. As luck would have it, I caught the ball. It looked like a thousand balls collapsing into themselves. Oh my God! I was tripping!

"By this time, it had gotten late and I had missed the ride to rehearsal in Philly with Frankie and Tony. Not wanting to miss practice, some friends drove me home to pick up some things. When I walked in the house, my mom asked what was going on. Still peaking on the acid, I looked at my mom and all I could see was her face undulating. It fuckin' freaked me out.

"At that point, my friends, who were waiting outside, drove me to the Marcus Hook train station. It turns out that what I thought was one tab of acid was actually closer to two. I was still feeling the effects big time. After my friends dropped me off, I was alone in the dark and scared as hell.

"When the train came and I got on, it was empty. All I wanted to do was find a seat and be left alone. Things in my mind's eye were still very distorted. At the next stop, an older man boarded the train and despite having dozens of empty seats available, he decided to sit right next to me. Still being in the throes of the acid, I turned to look out the window and in the reflection, this man was staring at me. His face was so distorted, it looked like it had caught on fire and they had put it out with a track shoe. I was freaking the fuck out.

"Finally arriving at the 15th Street station, I had to walk through the subway, three blocks, to get to our rehearsal space. The room we practiced in was about fifteen wide and fifty feet deep. When I entered the space, all I could see was Tony at the far end of the room, behind the drum kit, hitting his snare drum. I was so relieved to see familiar faces after a day of weirdness and paranoia. After sharing a good laugh, we proceeded to cancel rehearsal and call it a day—one hell of a day! My first acid trip. Thank God my mom looked a lot better when I got home."

JUST PRIOR TO the upcoming Temple Stadium concert, set for May 16, 1970, one of the local managers arranged for the guys to pick up Jimi Hendrix and The Experience at the Philadelphia airport in Tony's Vista Cruiser station wagon. Unfortunately, only the drummer, Mitch Mitchell, rode the wagon and, as Tony recalls, "was wearing these incredible knee-high laced boots."

"This is what a rock and roll star looks like!" remembered Tony.

The show at Temple Stadium led off with Cactus, followed by Ides of March, Grateful Dead, Steve Miller Band, and then Jimi Hendrix. Apparently, there was an issue with getting the Grateful Dead off the stage, forcing Steve Miller to cancel. Then,

Hendrix was stoned and had to be helped onto the stage. He was playing with one hand and just adjusting his knobs. The guys were so disappointed in Jimi, they headed off to rehearse.

According to an online source, this was the only concert ever held at the Temple Stadium venue. Then Chief of Police, Frank Rizzo, lived nearby and made certain to prevent a repeat of what he had termed a "hippie catastrophe."

AROUND THIS TIME, the band dropped Karen Young's managers, Paul and Jay and lost their rehearsal studio at 12th and Vine. So, they moved to the basement of the Dess Discount Store.

Tony was running Dess Discount stores, raising his family and painting a giant peace symbol on his backyard deck. Frankie was "experimenting." Their hair was growing long. One of the many jobs Tony gave Frank was painting the Dess building in Claymont. Frank did so using a one-inch brush. Workers across the street, at the Post Office, had a pool going to when he would finish. The building could have been sprayed in two or three days. Frank took three months. The band kept practicing.

Lacking confidence in their own vocals, they decided that they needed a lead singer, as well as a keyboard player, to complete their sound. They went through quite a few short-term keyboardists, as well as enlisting the services of a front man, now recalled only as "C.J." He could sing and had all the moves but was into shooting crystal.

The first Magic Band song was "Spoons of Crystal." Tony wrote about C.J.'s experiences with methamphetamines. Other original songs sung by C.J. included "Tell Me" and "Good Bye."

As the Magic Band, the group played C.J.'s former home, a mental institution. They set up in the cafeteria and rocked out to a couple hundred of the staff and patients of all ages. "Our first gig—we played stoner rock to dozens of drooling people in a mental institution," laughed Frank Ferrara.

In the days after that performance, one night C.J. exited a practice—and the band forever—running up the stairs while yelling, "You guys sound great! See you later." He was never heard from again.

Jimi Hendrix overdosed on September 18, 1970, while in England, only a few months after his Philadelphia performance. Alan Wilson, of Canned Heat, had passed weeks earlier, on the 3rd. Janice Joplin overdosed on heroin weeks later, on October 4th. All three were only 27—a rough year for the music industry.

FOR MORE THAN a year, the Magic Band only played live four times, instead working part-time, while writing and arranging what they intended to be their debut album. One day, Tony banged out a lick on a toy piano that ultimately became the opening melody for "Death of Country." The three wrapped into the mix other songs Frank and Frankie had been working on. With Tony into 'writing about death, pollution, the meaning of life, God, space, and time travel,' the trio came up with a number of songs: "Death of a Country," "Spoons of Crystal," and "Lord You Created a Mess." These were all intended to form the basis of a concept LP, *Death of a Country*.

"'No Trespassing' was about time travel," recalled Frank. "Tony was big into science fiction. 'My Window' was about being strapped in an electric chair, with only a little window to look out. It was one of my favorites."

"'Certainly Meaningless' did not have any meaning," recalled Frank. "It was just a combination of words that sounded cool. All of the lines meant nothing. 'Future Song' was about man being ready to touch the stars but now breeding in rusty cars. Man had destroyed the earth."

Eventually, they played a local gig at Rockford Park and people around town got to hear about the band and the new music they were creating.

It was during this "basement" period that they changed their name from the Magic Band (a name already being used by Captain Beefheart's band). Tony had been reading the just-issued March 4th, 1971, edition of *Rolling Stone*, when he came across the headline "The English Boom Is Over. Bang," a reference to the explosion of British bands that were causing a sensation in America. The word "BANG" leapt off the page at him and the Magic Band became BANG. "We wanted to find a name that was short and powerful," explained Frank Ferrara. "BANG was short, sweet, and to the point. It fit our music."

Although they were already planning their first album, they had nothing going for them except their desire to make it. "Eighteen months were spent in the basement," recalled Tony, "playing for ourselves and the kids who would be outside hanging around the metal sidewalk doors left open for air. The ceiling was so low, you had to duck pipes whenever you moved around. At times we would give a 'performance' for our friends, who would squeeze into the wall of sound and encourage us. We were learning how to write songs, building Voice of the Theater speakers for a sound system and dreaming of the things every band dreams. We were young, loud, and determined to make it!"

Frankie Gilcken was doing most of the lead singing in those days, harmonizing with Frank. Frankie brought drugs to the band but Frank and Tony liked their pot. Frankie stuck with the harder stuff and pushed things too far. One evening, he overdosed in an alley and was left for dead. Had Tony and Frank not found him and saved his life, BANG would have ended right there. So, having just turned seventeen and nearly dying, Gilcken was encouraged by the older Diorio to get out of Philadelphia before it killed him. But, at the time, BANG had little idea about how to promote themselves. Their hard rock approach hardly fit in with other musical events in Philadelphia and managers, record companies, and A&R men only came to the city to pursue the brand of sweet soul music that was becoming widely-known as the Philly Sound. However, there were one or two venues where they could play and it was as a result of this that they got an unexpected lucky break.

"The Anvil Inn was a bar that we went to in Kennett Square, Pennsylvania, that always had great live music," remembered Frankie. "The owners, Joe and Benny, loved us—one of our few gigs was their annual picnic with the band Euclid. One night, about a week after Jim Morrison died (Morrison died July 3, 1971), Tony started talking to the bass player of the band performing. He had overheard this guy say that he had been in the Classics IV, who had the hit 'Spooky.' Hey, this was big time— this guy had a hit! At some point in the conversation, the guy talked about a record distributor in Miami, Tone Distributors. They had a novelty hit going ('Window Washing Woman') and were looking for acts to sign.

"Within a week, Tony went to the bank and borrowed $1,000. We bought a tent, rented a trailer, packed up our equipment and headed down Interstate 95 in the Vista Cruiser to Miami."

Something was about to happen!

...

**"Man was great, he touched the stars
Now he breeds in rusty cars
Where once stood cities spiraling high
Now hangs death, a poisoned sky"**

—Lyrics from *Future Song*

Tony's parents, Teresa and Anthony Diorio.

Young Tony and at Staunton Military Academy.

Frank's '65 Mustang he spray painted purple to go to Woodstock.

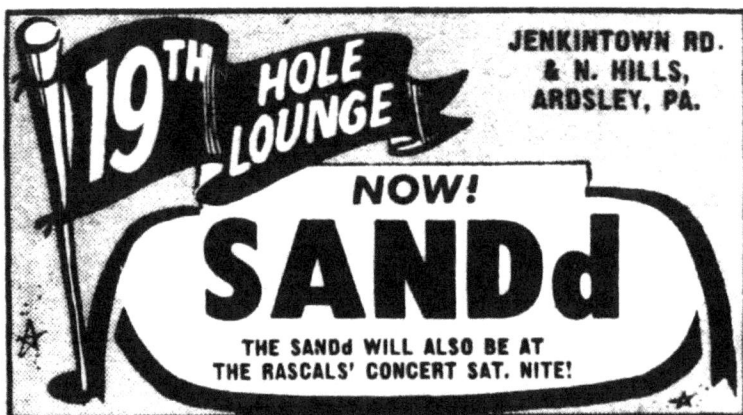

Sandd at the 19th Hole Lounge.

Sandd at the Living Room.

Sandd at the Spectrum with the Rascals.

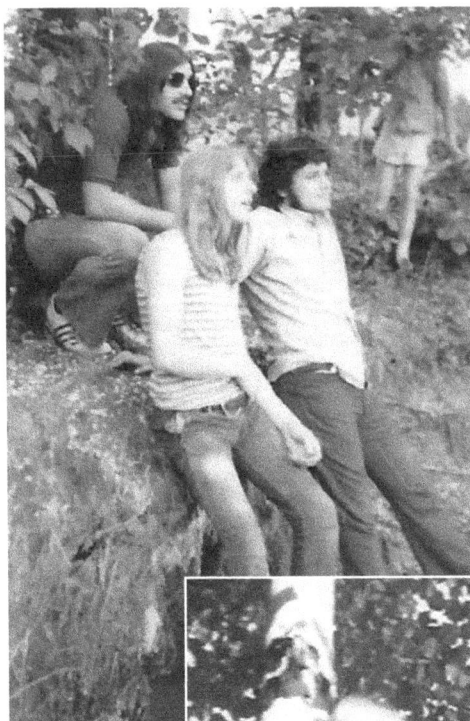

The Magic Band behind Tony's house, Spring 1970.

Magic Band performing at Rockford Park.

Above and below: Magic Band performing at Rockford Park.

Patty Hiner with Tony's kids: Kim, Anthony, and Michelle.

Tony painting a peace sign on his porch.

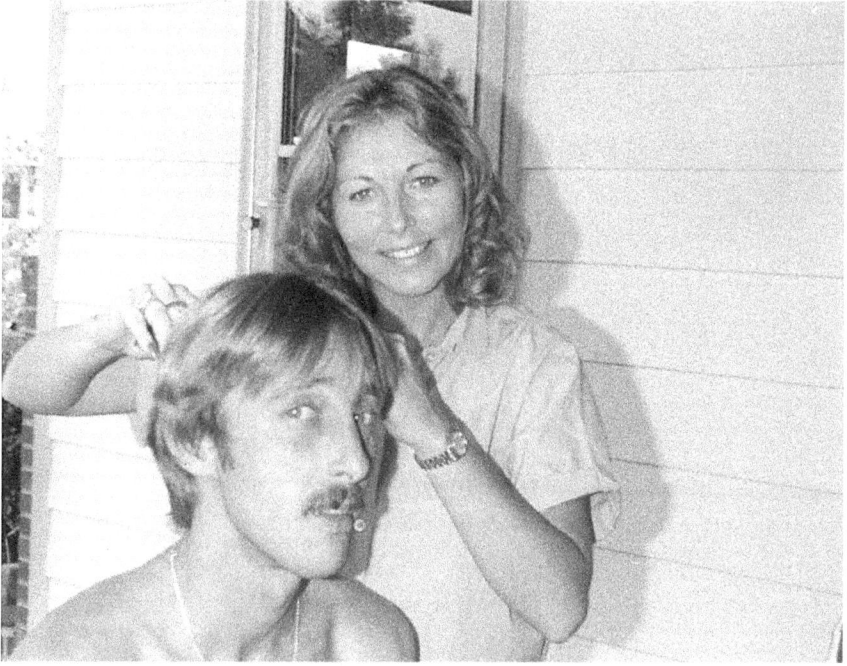

Jeanie Diorio cutting her cousin Steve Hiner's hair.

Steve and Jeanie in the kitchen of Tony's house in Claymont, Delaware.

HOT LABELS
HOT DISTRIBUTOR
HOT BREAK-OUT MARKET

TONE

DISTRIBUTORS, INC.

495 South East 10th Ct., Hialeah, Fla.

(305) 888-1685

HENRY STONE, Pres.

MURIEL STONE, Manager

Ad for Tone Distributors.

The Zep at Madison Square Garden: You can go to Haymarket & 8th Avenue and find five English roadies sit

'The English Boom Is Over. Bang.'

BY ANDREW BAILEY

LONDON—It started as a shot in the arm for the status of British musicians but for many it has ended up as an expensive pain in the ass: The Big Trip. The escape route from the sweaty English club circuit to the lusher pickings of America. The route has been well trodden. Last year the British Musicians' Union granted 76 permits to English

found out that in England the story is that the house record was smashed and the group went a bomb [smash].

"The days when just being English was good enough are long since over but it seems like a lot of people haven't cottoned on yet. But I'll say one thing about American promoters . . . they know how to look after you. At one place they gave me a whole galvanized bathtub of beer."

Webb's manager, Harry Simmonds, is one of the most experienced hands at exporting talent across the Atlantic. Another of his bands, Savoy Brown, with

in a group's evolution. "The bigger get in England the less places you play at. You can do a tour of all big concert halls here and be back ho in a week." That fact of life has Britain many of its biggest acts. B Faith played only one date in Brit Led Zeppelin and Jethro Tull are c rare visitors. Joe Cocker is a stranger

But there are signs that the situat is changing. Stratton Smith feels Europe is coming up fast as an alter tive to America. "I think that for middle rank of groups, Europe now c petes with America. Some of the b

Finding the name "BANG" in Rolling Stone, March 4, 1971.

BANG in the basement, early 1971.

Euclid at the Anvil Inn, July 1971.

CHAPTER 3

We're BANG from Philly

LEAVING PHILADELPHIA BEHIND, on July 19, 1971, BANG drove south on Interstate 95, towards Miami, stopping in Daytona Beach.

"On the way, we mailed out hundreds of post-cards to everyone from Walter Cronkite to Lassie, from Warner Brothers Records to Daffy Duck. Each postcard was stamped, 'BANG is in Miami,'" laughed Tony, "At Frankie's suggestion we went for a walk on the boardwalk. As we're hanging around, another long-haired freak, who looked a lot like us, came up and asked if we wanted to buy some grass. Frank bought an ounce (four fingers of Colombian Gold) for fifteen bucks. All we needed now were some rolling papers. **This is how the need for rolling papers launched our careers.**

"It was just about closing time, when we stopped for papers at a record store on the boardwalk in Daytona Beach. The manager had the key in the door, about to lock up, when we begged him to let us in. He did. Inside, we noticed a poster promoting a local *Battle of the Bands* competition," continued Tony. "We asked the manager of the shop if we could take part in the competition. He told us it was an old poster and the event had already taken place."

He mockingly told them that Rod Stewart and Faces and Deep Purple were playing in Orlando the following evening and "why didn't they go there and maybe they'll let you play!"

"This guy was busting our chops," said Tony." We spent that night in the tent getting high and discussing what had happened earlier. At some point, all red-eyed, I announced 'We're going to Orlando and play with Rod Stewart!'"

EARLY THE NEXT morning, the boys headed out for the hour-plus trek south to Orlando.

"What did we know? Ignorance is bliss!" recalled Frank. "We packed up the tent, climbed into the Vista Cruiser and headed to the next portal waiting for us in Orlando."

"At about noon, we pulled into the Orlando Sport Stadium. The gate was open, so we drove behind the auditorium," recalled Tony. "As we were walking in, sound company personnel were setting up the stage. They didn't even notice us, so we kept walking until we came to the first door, marked 'private.'

"We knocked and as the door opened, we announced, 'We're BANG from Philly and we're the best fucking band in the world and we want to play tonight!'"

"Where's your equipment?" the man inside asked.

Tony replied, "Right out in the U-Haul."

"Set it up," he said, "I wanna hear what you got."

We pulled the station wagon onto the middle of the floor and set up. After a few songs, he said, "You know what, you guys sound pretty good, plus you've got big balls. I'll let you open up the show tonight."

Tony continued, "This tall, thin guy was Rick Bowen, owner of East Coast Concerts. We can still see him standing in the middle of the empty arena watching us, arms folded, listening intently with his assistant Jimmy, as we played 'Death of a Country' and a few other songs. We were ready; all those months of practice, all those hours honing our craft, all the sacrificing each of us had done had prepared us for this moment in time. We passed the audition."

ON THE EVENING of July 21, 1971, as the crowd of 8,000 meandered into the auditorium in Orlando, Florida, BANG played songs from their unreleased *Death of a Country* album. The crowd was very encouraging.

Matthews Southern Comfort followed and then Deep Purple was next up, on their Fireball World Tour. Rod Stewart and Faces were the headliners. "Maggie May" had just entered the *Billboard 100* at 91, on its way to #1.

"After we performed our twenty-minute set and while the excitement of the night was still all over us, we had to go back out on stage and haul off our equipment in front of the crowd," recalled Tony. "We had no roadies. The shocked looks from the people down front watching us move our stuff was something to see."

"That show in Orlando was the beginning of our career," agreed Frank Ferrara. "Barely forty-eight hours after we left Philadelphia, we were opening the show for Rod Stewart and Faces and Deep Purple! This was only the fifth time in eighteen months that we had played anywhere except the basement."

Thinking they had done it all and feeling like their trip was a success, BANG was surprised when the promoter approached them and said he co-owned a hotel in Fort Lauderdale and wanted them to go there and wait for him.

"The Escape Hotel was a party place," recalled Frank. "For the next few days, that's what we did. When we met Rick at the airport, the first thing he said to us was 'How would you like to play with Steppenwolf in Richmond this weekend?' Was he kidding? Steppenwolf! 'Born to be Wild!' At that point, Rick Bowen became our manager.

"His company, East Coast Concerts, was a partner with Concerts West, which, at the time, was one of the biggest promoters in the country. Based out of Dallas, they booked all the super groups of the day. With East Coast and Concerts West as our managers, it meant we would be opening and touring with the top bands of that era. We were about to step onto the largest stages in the country with bands that were household names like Rod Stewart; Deep Purple; Steppenwolf; Guess Who; James Gang; Mountain; Ike & Tina; Fleetwood Mac; Cactus; Uriah Heep; Bloodrock; Dr. John; The Byrds; Alice Cooper; Allman Brothers; B.B. King; Chuck Berry; Three Dog Night; Black Sabbath; Emerson, Lake and Palmer; J. Giels Band; Billy Preston; Peter Frampton; Doobie Brothers; Yes; Nazareth; Jethro Tull; Joe Cocker; Savoy Brown; Bruce Springsteen; Bob Seger; Edgar Winter; Steve Miller; and Buddy Miles—that's how we started to build our fan base."

RICK BOWEN FIRST worked in 1967 as a concert producer for National Shows, Inc. in Charleston, West Virginia, where he earned his stripes on every type of arena event, including The Jefferson Airplane, The Ringling Brothers and Barnum Bailey

Circus, Holiday on Ice, Ice Capades, Loretta Lynn's Championship Rodeo, James Taylor, Led Zeppelin, Jesus Christ Superstar, Godspel, Mame, Kenny Rogers and the First Edition, Blood Sweat and Tears, Chicago, The Doors, Janis Joplin, The Four Seasons, War, The Temptations, and The Drifters. He also helped create the famous Royal Lipizzaner Stallion touring show, producing and promoting with the company's owners, brothers Phillip and Gary Lashinsky.

In 1969 Terry Bassett of Concerts West called and encouraged Rick to leave National Shows and move to Florida to set up a new company, East Coast Concerts, in partnership with him. In May of 1971 the owners of Fort Lauderdale's Escape Hotel, Bob Wickline and Phil Carnes, joined with Rick Bowen to form a new company, East Coast Concerts.

Rick was one of the pioneers of stadium rock concerts. He recognized this potential following the popularity of music festivals such as Woodstock and the Monterey Pop Festival. He thought there would be a money-making opportunity in staging concerts in more controlled environments. To this end, he and Concerts West convinced the management of Tampa Stadium to rent the 75,000-seat venue for a series of rock concerts. Three Dog Night, Led Zeppelin, Chicago, and Elton John subsequently appeared there in 1971.

The partners then moved onto Braves Stadium, in Atlanta, to run a similar series of concerts the following summer featuring Three Dog Night, Led Zeppelin, and Elton John. Following this, they expanded to a number of NFL stadiums across the country, including Irving Stadium, the home of the Dallas Cowboys. These were the first non-sports events held at most of these stadiums. In total, these partners produced more than 90% of the major rock concerts in Florida over a five-year period, 1969-1973.

REGARDING BANG, Rick Bowen had liked what he heard and hosted the guys at the Escape Hotel. Built in the late 40s and now more than 20 years old, the Escape was the first hotel in Fort Lauderdale to be open year-round and to feature a swimming pool.

Bowen officially became BANG's manager and began scheduling their performances as he had promised and it would be much more than just Steppenwolf!

The very first stop was a baseball stadium, Parker Field, in Richmond, Virginia, on Sunday, August 1, 1971. The venue was the home of the AAA Richmond Braves of the International League. It had a seating capacity of 9,500. The stage was set up on the pitcher's mound. The band's only surviving video is from this performance, as they opened for John Kay and Steppenwolf. At the time, "Born to Be Wild" was a mere three years old.

That Friday, BANG was off to Fayetteville, North Carolina, to open for the The Guess Who, at the Cumberland County Memorial Arena. Randy Bachman had been replaced by Kurt Winter and the band was promoting their *So Long, Bannatyne* and *The Best of the Guess Who* albums. Earlier in the week, Paul McCartney had announced the founding of Wings.

The next night, the two bands were joined by Gypsy at the Charlotte Coliseum, the home of the Carolina Cougars of the former American Basketball Association. The venue seated 8,500 and had been the site of Billy Graham crusades in the late 50s.

Gypsy had been the house band at the Whiskey A Go Go in West Hollywood, California, from September 1969 to April 1971. They were known for their *US Billboard Hot 100* single "Gypsy Queen Part 1 and 2."

The following Sunday, August 15, 1971, the Nixon administration announced new economic measures, including the elimination of the connection between gold and the dollar. At the Hollywood Sportatorium, near Miami, Florida, BANG opened for Three Dog Night, whose single "Liar" was at #4. The place was a hangar-like facility constructed out of concrete with a steel roof. Bereft of air conditioning, the bleacher seating could accommodate 14,000 sweltering fans. The concert was originally scheduled for nearby Pirate's World but Concerts West had its lease terminated by the venue due to complaints voiced to the town council, including potential fire code violations.

A week later on August 23, in West Palm Beach, Florida, the band joined up with The Edgar Winter Group, who was on their *White Trash* tour.

RICK BOWEN WAS also thinking about a record deal for the band. He decided to put up money to quickly record the album, *Death of a Country*. In a matter of several weeks, the band's dreams were all coming to fruition at once. It was almost too good to be true!

Rick decided the LP would be recorded independently and then hawked around to the major labels. Of course, BANG had already been working for many months on what they had intended to be their debut LP, *Death Of A Country* and so the songs were already pretty tight. This was just another case of a dream becoming reality.

"We went to Criteria Studios in Miami to start work on *Death Of A Country*," related Tony. "Ron and Howie Albert were our producers and engineers and they were great to work with."

The Albert Brothers, Ron and Howard, were widely-known for their association with Criteria Studios. Over the years, they helped produce or engineer over forty gold and thirty platinum records. The prior year, *Layla and Other Assorted Lovesongs* by Derek and the Dominoes was released, one of their prize achievements to that point. The piano played in *Layla* was in the studio when BANG arrived. Other artists who worked with the Alberts at Criteria before BANG were John Lee Hooker, Wilson Pickett, Allman Brothers Band, Aretha Franklin, Dr. John, Cactus, and The Rascals. Later, they would work with Black Oak Arkansas; Stephen Stills; Eric Clapton; Joe Walsh; Average White Band; James Gang; Bill Wyman; Crosby, Stills and Nash; Procol Harum; Harry Chapin; Tom Petty & The Heartbreakers; and many more.

Tony continued, "This was our first time in a recording studio and hearing our music played back loud on those big studio monitors was incredible. We knew *Death of a Country* so well that we were able to record it on the first take, with very few overdubs. At the time, Frankie was the lead singer and Frank sang mostly back-up. We used all kinds of effects on different songs, lots of panning and phasers. Originally, *Death of a Country* was conceived as a concept LP, so at the end of the album was a recording of the first atomic bomb blast at Yucca Flats. We tried it fast, slow, forwards, and backwards, trying to make it sound right. We finally settled on slow and backwards."

With *Death of a Country* complete by the end of August 1971, BANG's management started shopping the album and songs around.

SIX WEEKS LATER, Sunday, October 3, 1971, BANG was back on tour at the West Palm Beach Auditorium, in West Palm Beach, Florida, opening for Cactus, a band started by former Vanilla Fudge members, bassist Tim Bogart and drummer Carmine Appice, whom Tony idolized. Tickets were $3 in advance, $4 at the door.

That Thursday, October 7, *The French Connection*, starring Gene Hackman, premiered in theaters across the country. BANG was back at the Hollywood Sportatorium with Fleetwood Mac, who were on their *Future Games* tour. While Fleetwood Mac had added Christine McVie at this point, Stevie Nicks and Lindsay Buckingham were three years away. However, guitarist Bob Welch was with them at this time.

On Saturday the 9th, the band was at Curtis Hixon Hall in Tampa, Florida, to open for two Ike and Tina Turner shows that day. This 8,000-seat venue had just hosted, in April, the nationally televised light-heavyweight championship bout between Bob Foster and Ray Anderson. At the time, the Turners were at their peak, riding their cover of Creedence Clearwater Revival's "Proud Mary," which had been released in January. It reached #4 on the *Billboard Hot 100* and became the duo's best-selling single to date, selling well over a million copies. The following March, it won a Grammy Award. The song's parent album, *Workin' Together*, became their most successful studio release, peaking at #25 on the *Billboard 200*.

The 1971 touring season came to end on Saturday, October 30, when the band returned to the Cumberland County Memorial Arena in Fayetteville, North Carolina, to appear with Mountain and The J. Geils Band. Leslie West and Mountain had been riding two gold LPs and their hit song "Mississippi Queen," which peaked at #25 the prior year. The J. Geils Band had released two albums in 1971 and had yet to have a top single. Their commercial success was a few years away.

While BANG was doing their sound check, Leslie West, of Mountain, was listening. He noticed Frankie's Les Paul had mini-humbuckers. He suggested a full humbucker would make his guitar sound better. Leslie then asked one of the roadies to take the pickup from his flying v and give it to Frankie, which he did.

...

**"Keep abreast of turmoiled times
Prudent people mouth their lines
Watch them work at being not
Pump their ears make them hot"**

—Lyrics from *Certainly Meaningless*

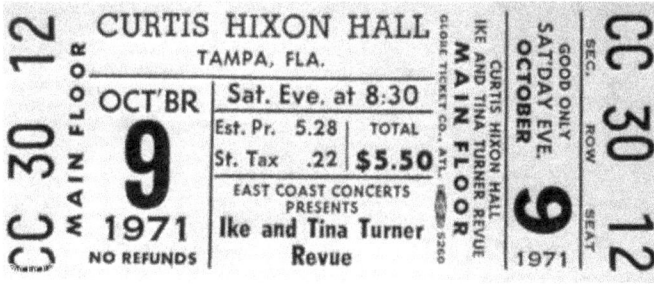

Ike & Tina ticket stub, October 9, 1971.

Zig-Zag rolling papers.

The Escape Hotel, Ft. Lauderdale, Florida.

BANG at Richmond Stadium with Steppenwolf,
August 1, 1971.

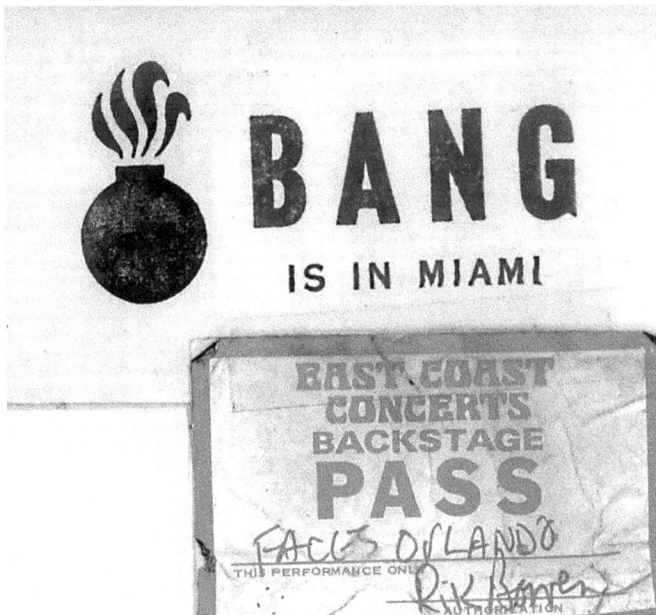

BANG is in Miami / Faces backstage pass.

BANG outside Criteria Studios, August 1971.

BANG in the field outside Criteria Studios.

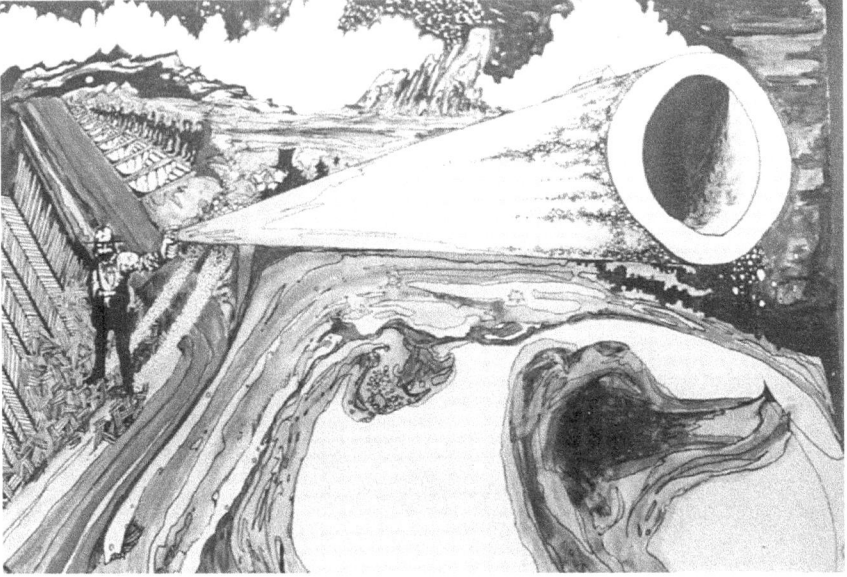

Original *Death of a Country* cover.

Final *Death* cover with BANG in the barrel.

Above and below: BANG doing vocals on *Death of a Country* at Criteria Studios.

Backstage before Rock Spectacular at the Hollywood Sportatorium.

BANG fireworks at the Hollywood Sportatorium.

BANG at the Hollywood Sportatorium.

Tony, 1972.

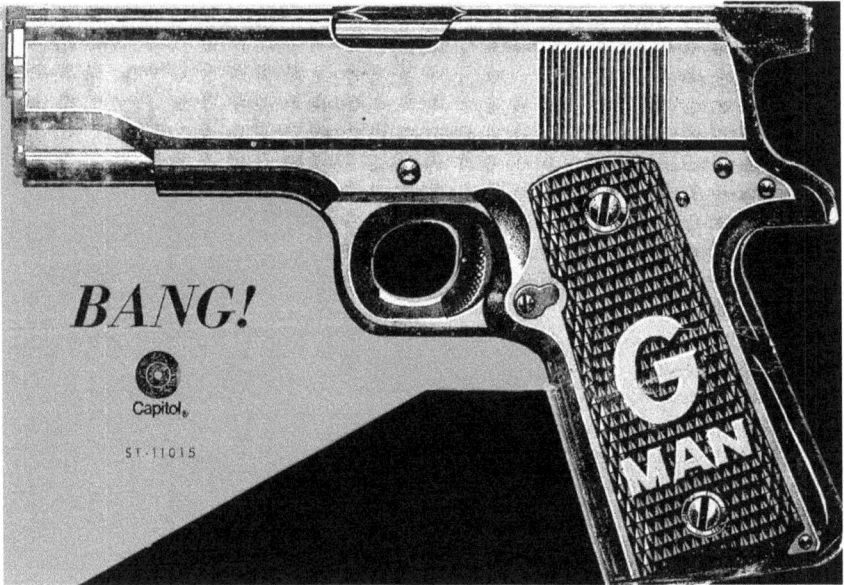

G-Man promotion.

BANG outside a friend's house in Fayetteville, North Carolina.

CHAPTER 4

BANG!

LATE IN 1971, a deal was struck with Capitol Records for four albums thanks to Rick Bowen being well-connected with Midge, who was the secretary to the vice president of Capitol Records, Herb Belkin. The band was ecstatic.

"This was it," said Tony Diorio, "A deal with the label the Beatles were on."

Everything seemed to be falling into place except that the band had been signed on the strength of *Death of a Country* and Capitol had decided to reject the album. According to Frank, the record label "didn't want to release *Death of a Country* because they thought a heavy concept album would go over peoples' heads." Instead, Capitol requested that the band come up with a less raw, more commercial offering. Thus, it was that BANG's great opening statement, *Death of a Country*, was left on the shelf. It would be another twenty-eight years before the album would eventually see the light of day. The important thing, though, was that Capitol wanted the band.

That November, the label brought in producer Michael Sunday, who had overseen the fourth, self-titled, Blue Cheer album and, therefore, had all the right credentials to handle a heavy metal power trio. "I was looking for a working band, one that was touring," said Michael. He flew down to Florida to see the band at the Sportatorium in Miami. He felt BANG was a solid act to work with—not spectacular but with potential.

Jimmy Ienner, an executive for CAM USA, the music publisher, had heard Frank scream "people turning me around" in the song "Death of a Country," and emphatically suggested that Ferrara be the lead singer. Thus, Sunday changed the band's lead vocalist, pointing out that Frank looked like a hard rock lead singer and should therefore take that role. He also listened to *Death of a Country*, after which he said that he was going away for a couple of weeks and that they needed to write a new album before he returned. He told them he wanted to capture a sound like Black Sabbath, Led Zeppelin, and Grand Funk Railroad. And that was what they did, in only ten days.

According to Tony, "When Mike Sunday came back after two weeks, we went back into Criteria Studios and started recording the *BANG* album. The band worked on the album until January (1972). The first day was spent perfecting Frankie's guitar sound. Initially, Frankie had a Traynor amp when we did *Death of a Country* but he was now using Marshalls. His speaker bottom was moved around from place to place, inside and outside and finally ended up in a bathroom with a mike in front of it. Mike Sunday basically got the sound—you know—the heavy metal sound. He inspired us."

"Those were the days when everything was experimental," said Karl Richardson, the engineer. "We were looking for something more reverberant. We didn't want BANG to sound like everybody else. In those days, records were more like paintings, than photographs. The studio was a palette and we were always thinking about art—not just taking a picture." The team of Ron and Howie Albert, and Karl are best known for their later work on the Bee Gees' *Saturday Night Fever* LP. Apparently Barry Gibb was inspired by the sound of driving over a nearby bridge, resulting in the rhythm of "Stayin' Alive."

With Sunday in the driver's seat, BANG had a tighter, more disciplined feel than the rawer, slightly meandering *Death of a Country*, with only "The Queen" breaking the five-minute barrier. The psychedelic-era hangover, that had seen the band experimenting with studio effects, was jettisoned in favor of a leaner, meaner sound, with Frank's lead vocals—pitched midway between Ozzy Osbourne and Robert Plant—complementing Frankie's Iommi-inspired fretwork, to give the band an even more pronounced Black Sabbath vibe, particularly on "Come With Me" and "Future Shock" (the latter inspired by Alvin Toffler's hugely influential book of the same name). The song "Come With Me" was written in response to Tony's curious questions to

Frankie about doing drugs. Nevertheless, the songs, melodies, and riffs were strong enough to ensure that BANG was far more than the work of a surrogate Sabbath.

"Last Will And Testament" and "Our Home" were outstanding compositions, with Frankie's wistful harmony work reflecting the relative subtleties of the songs, while "Redman" and the superb "Questions" were tight, catchy little rockers that seemed to have considerable commercial potential.

"I thought it was a good record," said Michael Sunday, "very workmanlike—not spectacular but really good. The guys were hard working and very competent. Blue Cheer, at the time, were two drug addicts and a health-food nut. BANG was a real pleasure to work with."

One night, the band and Sunday were walking back to the hotel after recording and enjoying some weed, when they were stopped by a two policemen. Sunday, the producer, was the more reputable person in the group, the three band members being longhairs. "We're just having a meeting of the minds," explained Sunday to law enforcement. The cops let them go and all was well.

"We were very pleased with the record," said Frank. "I remember all of us getting high and listening to the playback for the first time. The opening notes of the first track, 'Lions, Christians,' sounded awesome. We were lucky to have a great producer in Michael Sunday. He helped us to create our own sound."

On January 2nd, Frank flew to Los Angeles where he was picked up by Michael on his motorcycle. The two rode to the Capitol Tower where Frank redid the lead vocals to "Our Home" and "The Queen." It was Frank's first trip to Hollywood, lasting only a couple days.

THE FIRST LIVE performance of the new material from the BANG album was performed in Tallahassee, Florida, on Friday, January 28, 1972. Two weeks later on the 11th, BANG performed with Uriah Heep, Cactus, and The Damnation of Adam Blessing at the, now familiar, Hollywood Sportatorium, near Miami, Florida. Heep's iconic *Demons and Wizards* LP was nearing release, which included the single "The Wizard." The *Fort Lauderdale News* carried a story about the Rock Spectacular featuring the four bands. Concerning BANG, the paper said:

"Third on Rock Spectacular is a brand new Capitol Records group called BANG. BANG is a Philadelphia power trio. The group's first album, entitled *BANG*, is being rushed for release to coincide with its appearance on Rock Spectacular.

BANG has appeared on the bill with some very well-known names, Three Dog Night, Guess Who, Steppenwolf, Rod Stewart and Faces, Deep Purple, and others. It was their dynamic stage show that literally led them to their recording contract with Capitol.

Lead guitarist Frank Gilcken moves and jumps all over the stage as the group hits with song after song of get-it-on music. Gilcken usually appears in a white silk tuxedo and corresponding top hat worn over a Mickey Mouse shirt."

VALENTINE'S DAY 1972 was a Monday. Richard Nixon was preparing his famous trip to China. Capitol Records released the *BANG* album (Capitol Records, ST-11015).

"We never got a copy of the album when it was released," complained Frank Ferrara, "I had to go down to Sid's on Sunrise Boulevard where they had a BANG display in the window. I had to spend seven dollars to buy a copy of our own album."

Capitol initially pulled out all the stops when it came to promoting the album. It was housed in a memorable sleeve design that featured some Roy Lichtenstein-like pop-art lettering of the band's name. The imagery was taken from the original artwork by David O'Hara for the unpublished *Death of a Country* album. As Tony explained, though, the finished article wasn't quite what the band had been expecting.

"Originally the artwork had an ink drawing of the three of us in the gun barrel. Capitol's art department came up with the cartoon-like BANG explosion which proved to be eye-catching and still remembered today worldwide. We expected the cover to be a gatefold with this great futuristic painting in the inside of 'mankind breeding in rusty cars.'

"Moving from Philly to Ft. Lauderdale was an incredible change of environment to start our careers," continued Tony. "Our manager, Rick Bowen, introduced us to conch chowder from Ernie's in Miami, which we visited many times. One night, all of us, roadies Steve Hiner and Danny Simmonds, and road manager Tommy Wingate were driving there in two cars when suddenly our music came over the radio. We rolled down the windows, music blaring, screaming with excitement from car to car. This was the first time we heard our music on the radio—something sweet that only happens once. Fort Lauderdale and Miami were rotating cuts from our album heavily, since that's where we lived. Once, we were walking out of the Escape Hotel, where we were staying and could just barely hear 'Future Shock' playing in this hippie van coming up the street. What a trip as it got louder and zoomed past us!"

Frank recalled an important contribution from Danny, who was living with the band. "One night, we probably smoked an entire bag of weed," said Frank. "The whole time, Danny was drawing a poster of us in concert, making little dots with number-two pencils. It was amazing. Danny also drew the BANG girl image later on."

BANG started climbing the US album charts, selling over 80,000 copies of the LP.

ON WEDNESDAY, MARCH 1, 1972, BANG was back in Fayetteville, North Carolina, to play with Black Sabbath, who was in the midst of their *Master of Reality Tour*. Wild Turkey was to open this evening, followed by the boys from Philly.

That afternoon, the band was hanging out with Ozzy Osbourne and Geezer Butler from Black Sabbath. They offered to introduce them to cheesesteaks, having discovered a sandwich shop in town that was attempting to replicate their favorite Philadelphia cuisine.

"I've never had a bloody cheesesteak," admitted Ozzy.

And so BANG introduced the Prince of Darkness to the delicacy. After chomping on a few bites, he asked, "I have another question for you. What do the fans mean when they are making the "V" signs with their fingers? For our Churchill, it meant victory."

"To them it means one of two things," answered Frankie. "It either means peace or boogie."

After that, Ozzy would often be seen on stage flashing dual V-signs to all of his audiences, as captured on the cover of their next album *Vol. 4*.

Said Tony, "We were in North Carolina, opening for Black Sabbath. Here we are, playing with our heroes! We had been using a shotgun to open our show but we blew out all or part of the sound system twice, probably because the sound-man had not turned off the mikes. We stopped ending the show with a shotgun because of a mishap near my head when Steve, our roadie, who was waiting to hand the gun to me, had too heavy a finger on the trigger.

"We were one of the first groups to use fireworks. At the end of our set, I had the double bass drums going into this cymbal crescendo. The music was just building up and up. Our roadie Steve lit the fireworks display over the top of my head as it spelled out "BANG"—burning red, then blue, and then white, until it turned into smoke. When it went off, the whole audience—about 15,000 people—stood up and started rushing the stage. I mean, this just blew their minds. They were wild-eyed.

"It wasn't widely known that I had to pay off the fire marshal," said Rick Bowen. "The fireworks filled the stadium with smoke. It was pretty intense."

As the band was leaving town the next day, a radio DJ, who was at the show, said the underdog group, BANG, stole the show.

"It's something to have idols that you look up to. It's another thing to play with your idols. And it's an even greater thing to steal the show!" continued Tony.

BANG never opened for Black Sabbath again but Ozzy never stopped holding up the dual "V" signs.

THE FIRST FEW weeks of March 1972 saw BANG with Yes in Columbia, South Carolina, on the 3rd, followed by a gig with James Gang in Birmingham, Alabama, on the 10th and a performance with The Byrds in Virginia Beach on the 15th, Frank's 19th birthday. Yes had released its double-platinum album *Fragile* the prior November and the song "Roundabout" was on the airwaves. Joe Walsh's James Gang had recently released *Thirds* and were seeing a lot of action from the song "Walk Away." The veteran Byrds, sans David Crosby, were promoting their recent release, *Farther Along*. This was the week the movie *The Godfather* was released in theaters.

The concert on March 17, 1972, was somewhat controversial. The band was at the Richmond Arena in Richmond, Virginia, with Mitch Ryder and the Detroit Wheels, Bruce Springsteen, and the Mike Quatro Jam Band. The order of performance was billed as Springsteen, BANG, Quatro, and then Mitch Ryder, each allotted about an hour and a half. However, Ryder actually performed before Quatro. The venue had a capacity of 6,500 but the promoter attempted to address the echo and intimacy problems by reducing the seating to 4,500 and rotating the stage a quarter turn against the center wall. The stage was enlarged to permit two bands to be set up simultaneously, in an effort to reduce time between acts. Unfortunately, the turnout was only about 1,000. A review of Springsteen's performance mentioned the wide variety of styles in his set. He had just been signed by Columbia Records and had not yet recorded an album.

The next day, the 18th, the band was in Miami to play with Seatrain and It's a Beautiful Day at the Hollywood Sportatorium. Seatrain was a mildly successful American fusion band nearing the end of its run.

Sunday March 26, 1972, BANG was back to the Charlotte Coliseum to play with Deep Purple, Nazareth, and Buddy Miles. Deep Purple's *Machine Head* was released the day before, containing the iconic "Smoke on the Water," as well as "Highway Star." The album later went double platinum in the US. Nazareth was a couple years away from releasing *Hair of the Dog* and Buddy Miles was popular for his connections to the late Jimi Hendrix.

On April Fool's Day 1972, all major league baseball exhibitions were canceled due to a strike. It was the first time games had been called for this reason. This first baseball strike interrupted the end of spring training and delayed the start of the season until April 15. This day, a Saturday, BANG was at the Tangerine Bowl in Miami, Florida, to warm up for the upcoming Mar Y Sol concert in Puerto Rico. Blood Rock, Potliquor, and Dr. John & Heaven were on the bill for what was promoted as an "Easter Spectacular."

At the beginning of March, Potliquor had started a six-week tour with Bloodrock and Cactus with a break in the schedule to appear at the Mar Y Sol Pop Festival in Puerto Rico on April 1–3, 1972. Other notable artists appearing at this festival were Alice Cooper; the Allman Brothers Band; B. B. King; Billy Joel; Brownsville Station; Cactus; Dave Brubeck; Emerson, Lake and Palmer; Faces; the J. Geils Band; Long John Baldry; Herbie Mann; and the Mahavishnu Orchestra with John McLaughlin.

A ticket stub for the concert featuring Cactus, Bloodrock, Potliquor, and Dr. John and Heaven at the Tangerine Bowl, located at 1610 West Church Street in Downtown Orlando,

Florida, was dated April 1, 1972. The face value was $4 and the show began at 1:00 p.m. Cactus was an American hard rock and blues band formed in 1969, in New York. They were known as "the American Led Zeppelin." Bloodrock was an American hard rock and blues band from Fort Worth, Texas, that enjoyed considerable success from 1969 to 1975. Potliquor was a Southern Rock band from Baton Rouge, Louisiana, that formed in 1969 and disbanded in 1979. Dr. John, the stage name of Malcolm John "Mac" Rebennack, is an American multi-instrumentalist whose music blended New Orleans blues, jazz, rock, et al.

Before the performance, the band was backstage with Dr. John, who was kicked back in a chair, sound asleep, moments before he was to go on. Frankie noticed he was napping and made a comment that stirred Mr. Rebennack. "When you've been doing it as long as I have, you learn how to relax," said Dr. John in a real cool voice. He then got up and went out on stage and proceeded to kick ass.

That night BANG's manager, Rick Bowen, wanted to surprise the band by chartering a plane to take them to Puerto Rico. He invited a few friends and Herb Belkin, Vice President of Capitol and his wife to come along.

"My plane wasn't able to carry the load—all of the people and equipment. My pilot had an old DC3," said Rick Bowen, who was co-piloting, "but the interior was in the shop. So, there were no seats—just some sofas bolted to the floor. We barely cleared the smokestacks as we flew out of Fort Lauderdale, we were so heavy."

Frank recalled, "The plane that he got was from World War 2 and was being refurbished and wasn't done yet. It had no seats but two sofas to sit on. It also didn't have a bathroom. We had to use a Kentucky Fried Chicken box between blankets—not enough room for everyone to sit, so we ended up sitting on the floor of the plane. A normal flight to Puerto Rico from Ft. Lauderdale usually takes a couple of hours. It took us four hours. The plane could only fly so high and we ended up running into a huge storm. To entertain ourselves, we were telling stories about all the lost planes and ships in the Bermuda Triangle, as we were flying over it. Suddenly, we began losing altitude. The plane just dropped for about 30 seconds. Talk about fear! The plane had no lights inside and all we could hear was thunder and lightning. It was pitch black. We eventually regained altitude and proceeded on our way. When we finally landed, one of the front tires went flat as we were coming to a stop. At that point, the doors opened and everyone in the plane ran for the weeds, because nobody was gonna use that Kentucky Fried Chicken bucket."

"There was barely enough room to land given how heavy we were. We had to land so hard and fast, we hit the brakes and blew out a tire," recalled Rick, "I had prepaid for a truck to meet us at the airport when we arrived. They left the truck but took the keys. Steve and Danny loaded the truck anyway and hot-wired it."

"The plane sat at the end of the runway for two days and was the topic of discussion among the acts performing," recalled Tony, "The hotel was upscale, so it was all of these long-haired freaks and these button-down money people. We were to fly from the hotel to the concert site over the jungle via helicopter. Wow!"

Saturday evening, before their performance, the band ventured out to attend the concert. They were not allowed to go on the helicopter at that point and did not have the keys to the truck. So, they hot-wired it again and drove it down the jungle road to the venue.

"As we approached," recalled Frank, "Emerson, Lake and Palmer was playing 'Lucky Man.' As we got closer, the song became louder and louder. 'Oh what a lucky man, he was!' It gave me chills."

AROUND NOON ON Easter Sunday, April 2, 1972, BANG played in Puerto Rico at the Mar Y Sol concert with Alice Cooper; Emerson, Lake and Palmer; Billy Joel; and many more. That Sunday was a very hot day and BANG played without cover under direct sunlight. Tony remembered the cymbals being so hot, they burned his finger on touch. Frank remembered Tony spitting on the cymbal and it sizzling like your brain on drugs.

Black Sabbath was scheduled to be there but never performed after being stuck on the road on the last day. Overall, the festival was criticized in the papers. The venue was about 30 miles west of San Juan near the town of Manati adjacent to Los Tubos beach. Over 30,000 attended and there were accidental deaths at the beach and a murder. The promoter, Alex Cooley, escaped an arrest warrant by leaving the island.

Following is a list of the bands who performed at Mar Y Sol:

- Allman Brothers Band
- Long John Baldry
- Banda del K-rajo
- BANG
- Brownsville Station
- Dave Brubeck w/Gerry Mulligan
- Cactus
- Alice Cooper
- Jonathan Edwards
- Elephant's Memory
- Emerson, Lake and Palmer
- Faces w/ Rod Stewart
- Fran Ferrer y Puerto Rico 2010
- J. Geils Band
- Billy Joel
- Dr. John the Night Tripper
- B.B. King
- Mahavishnu Orchester w/ John McLaughlin
- Herbie Mann
- Nitzinger
- Osibisa
- Michael Overly
- David Peel and the Lower East Side
- Potliquor
- Rubber Bank
- Stonehenge

The Puerto Rico performance was the first major appearance for Billy Joel, who had released his first album, *Cold Spring Harbor*, a few months prior.

For BANG, the escape from Puerto Rico was almost as harrowing as the flight over. After the show was over, the owners of the truck showed up and were very upset. They decided they wanted more money and wanted to hold the equipment hostage. After involving the police, they negotiated to get the equipment on the truck and to the airport.

While Rick and the band continued to argue with the local truck owners, the roadies quietly drove past the hotel, heading for the plane. After stalling as long as possible, the guys then jumped into a waiting taxi and sped to the airport. The islanders quickly followed, jumping into their vehicle. They were a minute behind.

As the guys arrived at the airport, the roadies were just finishing loading the plane. They exited the taxi, jumped on the plane and slammed the door shut, just as the natives arrived and retrieved their truck.

"As we were getting ready to taxi out of Dorado," remembered Rick, "the Puerto Ricans parked in front of the plane and got on top of the truck. We fired up the engines. The DC3 props were gigantic. Bill proceeded to rev the props, advancing towards the truck. Terrified, the guys jumped in and moved."

The band mates then watched out the windows as the truck, with angry natives waving their arms, chased the plane but were left in its dust. Meanwhile, the Capitol executives and other friends decided to take a proper plane home and weren't on the return trip on the rustic DC3.

BACK ON SOLID ground, the band was quickly off to Atlanta, Georgia, for a performance with The Guess Who at Municipal Auditorium, on April 5th.

After the concert, late at night, the band was riding back to Fort Lauderdale on Interstate 70, heading south. "Danny, our roadie, was driving the Vista Cruiser with Frankie in the front seat," recalled Frank. "Me, Tony, and Steve Hiner were in the back sleeping. All of a sudden, out of nowhere, we were startled by Danny screaming 'HOLD ON!' Looking up, all we could see were sheets of rain pounding us. We couldn't see anything else! Apparently, the U-Haul started to hydroplane, whipping us into a full 360 spin at 70 miles per hour. We spun four or five times before we ended up smashing into a guard rail, where we came to a stop.

"When we got out of the car, we were facing north. The back door of our trailer was jarred open and some equipment had spilled out on to the highway."

As they climbed out of the Vista Cruiser, in the pouring rain, Frankie realized something was wrong. "I can see my eyebrow!" he said. Apparently he had hit his forehead against the dash and now needed a face adjustment.

"How nobody was seriously injured," said Frank, "I'll never know. Right behind us, a tractor trailer driver pulled over to make sure we were okay. He told us how incredible it was that we were able to not hit anything while we were spinning. Amazingly, the gods of rock n' roll were looking out for us. It just so happened that Rick and Tommy Wingate were a few minutes behind us and we joked that we should all lay down and play dead and have Rick find us that way. Again we escaped a perilous situation and were able to get back home to Ft. Lauderdale before heading to our next show in Baton Rouge.

BANG rejoined The Guess Who for shows in Baton Rouge, Louisiana, on the 7th and Shreveport, Louisiana, on the 8th.

In the span of one week, the boys played five shows and nearly died twice!

THE FOLLOWING WEEK, BANG appeared with Joe Cocker at the Moody Coliseum in Dallas, Texas, on April 11. This was followed by two shows with James Gang on the 15th and 16th at Will Rogers Coliseum in Fort Worth and then a show in Tulsa, Oklahoma. Little did the band know, they were peaking. On Monday, April 17, 1972, the *BANG* LP was at #157 on the *Billboard 200* and the 45 hit #99.

The *BANG* album received positive reviews from the era's pundits, with *Billboard* commenting that the band "on first listen, sounds incredibly like Led Zeppelin . . . they play at the same frenetic pace as Zeppelin and Frank Ferrara's vocals are so similar to those of Robert Plant's, as to be downright amazing." Bolstered by such comments, suddenly, it seemed, the band were on their way to stardom.

The success of the album was cemented by the release of arguably the most contagious track, "Questions," as a single (Capitol Records, 3304). It was climbing on the *Billboard* singles chart (according to Frank Ferrara, it also reached the No. 2 spot in Hong Kong)—a performance that vindicated the band's faith in the song, which apparently hadn't been shared by their producer.

"When Michael Sunday told us that we had to write a new album in two weeks, he said that he wanted it to sound like a mixture of Black Sabbath, Led Zeppelin, and Grand Funk Railroad," recalled Frankie Gilcken. "But when he returned and we played 'Questions' to him, he said that he didn't like it and that it didn't fit in with the rest of the album. Eventually, though, he agreed to let us include it on the LP. Capitol then decided to release it as a single."

"It just goes to show that, most times, the band knows what's best when it comes to their own music," said Tony. "I wrote 'Questions' at the place we were staying, the Escape Hotel. I remember writing it sitting up against the wall, with a mattress on the floor. We were high. At least I was!"

Tony believes that the song could have been a much bigger hit had Capitol really thrown their weight behind it. "'Questions' could have been in the top ten, if not the top five, because there was a point there when they stopped working it."

AFTER A SHORT respite, the band was back on the road for a concert with Cactus in Charleston, South Carolina, at County Hall on April 29. This was followed up with three dates with Alice Cooper. The first was May 5 at the Convention Center Arena, also known as the Hemis Fair Arena, in San Antonio, Texas. Canned Heat also appeared. The next night, the bands were at the Memorial Auditorium in Dallas, Texas. Then, on the 7th, they went to Houston, Texas, to the Hofheinz Pavilion, an 8,500-seat venue on the University of Houston campus. There Blue Öyster Cult, who had recently released their debut album, joined them. Canned Heat continued to ride the popularity of their top hit, "Going Up the Country," which had become the unofficial Woodstock anthem. Alice Cooper had just released the week prior the iconic hit "School's Out," His stage show featured a boa constrictor hugging Cooper on-stage, the murderous axe chopping of bloodied baby dolls and execution by hanging at the gallows.

BANG stayed in Houston an extra day on May 8, 1972, to appear on the popular Larry Kane Show but were at it again at a benefit concert at Northeast High School in Fort Lauderdale, Florida, on May 10.

DICK HORTON, OF the *Delaware County Times*, based in Chester, Pennsylvania, wrote an article on May 24th about the hometown band. "If you overhear your teenager talking about BANG," wrote Horton, "they're not about to commit a crime or try a new drug. BANG is a new rock group whose first record album was released in February. The trio are all area residents."

Anthony Diorio, Tony's father, was interviewed by Horton and reported sales of 69,000 copies of the first album. "Capitol Records is putting a lot of promotion into the group," said the elder Diorio. "Two weeks ago, the record was released on the international market. Full page ads are appearing in national recording magazines."

The senior Diorio reported the record was selling well at his discount stores. "Of course things have changed," he said. I ran a newspaper advertisement for the record and offered autographed copies. Although sales were boosted, no one asked for the autograph. The main thing wrong with our generation, is that our music doesn't say anything. It was all 'moon and spoon.' Today, the lyrics have a story to tell."

Horton reported the album had climbed to #170 on *Billboard*'s top 200 list, rising nine positions. "According to Jim Farrow at the Tri-State Mall Record Store," wrote Horton, "the first dozen copies were gone within an hour. A second order of fifty was reduced by one half in two days. Since then, the store has reordered several times, each time completely selling out within days."

"A couple members of the group hung out in here a lot," said Farrow. "Even still, it's rare for any record to approach those sales."

THE NEXT NIGHT, the band performed at Fort Bragg, North Carolina, as the guests of a Lt. General John H. Hay, to participate in *Harmony Through Music*. The Howard Hager Trio, Jimmy Witherspoon and War, Loretta Lynn and Conway Twitty, Jerry Butler, Anthony Armstrong Jones, and others played in addition to BANG.

"I remember coming into dinner at the officer's club," recalled Frankie. "The general was like John Wayne. As the three of us long hairs walked in and were to sit at the head table, all of the officers stood and saluted us. It was very surreal."

"Some of the officers thought Frankie was a hot little chick because of his long hair," laughed Frank. "They were flirting with him and trying to get him into their bunks. Meanwhile, the other guys were telling us war stories about all the 'VC' they had killed in Vietnam. It was a very odd situation, to say the least."

THE TOUR ENDED with an appearance with Seatrain and Ted Nugent's Amboy Dukes in Jacksonville, Florida on June 3rd.

...

"Happy people make their way
Thru the world everyday
Saddened people, they can't seem to find
Their way across the rejected line"

—Lyrics from *Last Will and Testament*

COSMIC PRODUCTION PRESEN
Cactus, Bloodrock, Potlic
Dr. John and Heaver

APRIL

1

1972
NO REFUND

SUNSHINE
CONCERTS 1:

— ADVANCE S
Est. Pr. 3.84
St. Tax   .16

TANGERINE
ORLANDO, F

Stub from concert at the Tangerine
Bowl, April 1, 1972.

BOOGIE!

...'till the Band breaks down.

Richmond Arena
Fri. March 17th 7pm
Mitch Ryder and Detroit
Bang -•- *Bruce* Springsteen Band
Special Guest Star Mike Quatro Jamband

TICKET LOCATIONS: *Music City, Southside Plaza* ALL TICKETS $3.50
Gary's Willow lawn · The Store in the fan · W-G-O-E

Poster for show with Bruce Springsteen on
March 17, 1972.

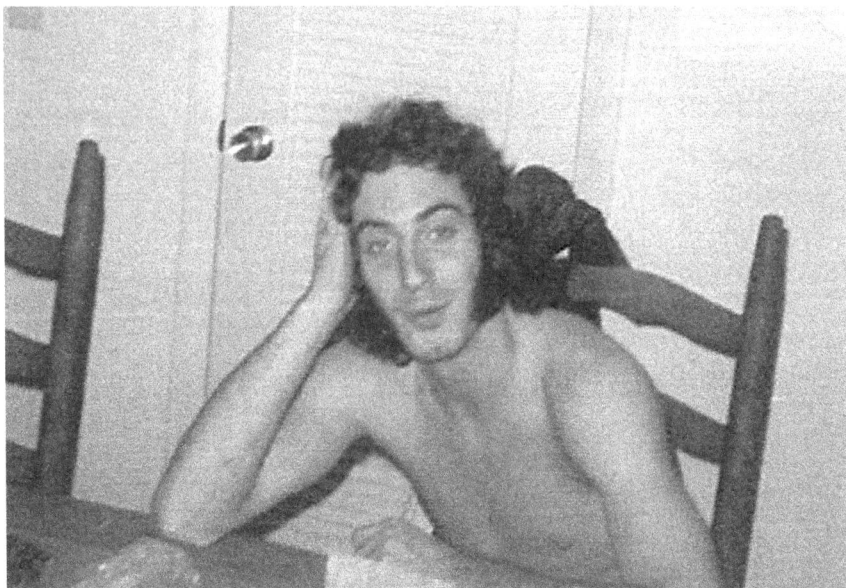

Danny Simmonds at BANG's apartment, April 1972.

Danny Simmonds and Frank Gilcken.

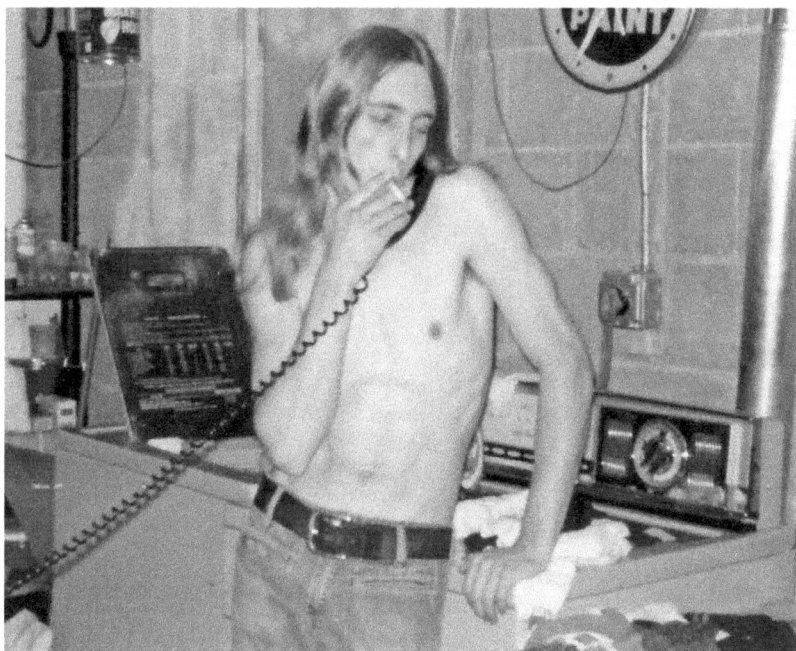

Steve Hiner.

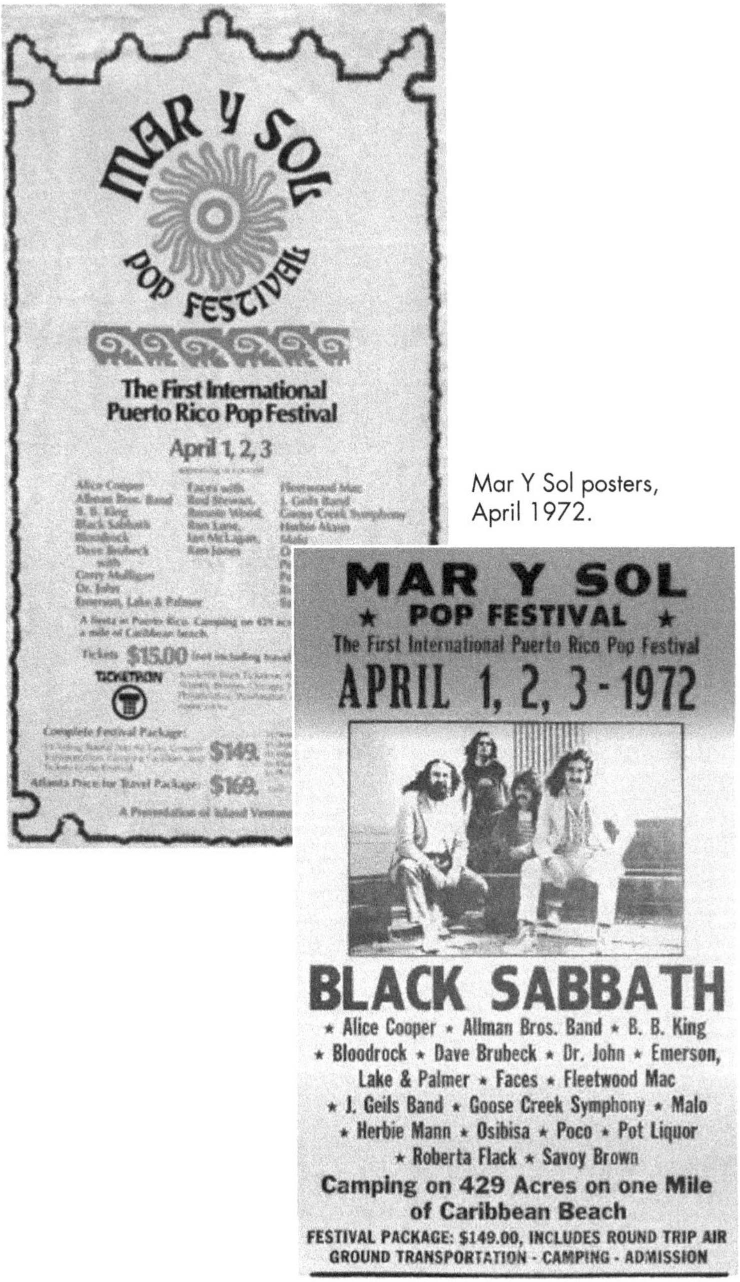

Mar Y Sol posters, April 1972.

Ad and stubs from Alice Cooper concerts, May 1972.

Frankie, Tony, and Frank

Record chart for local Delaware radio station, April 1972.

Questions sheet music.

Questions single and sleeve.

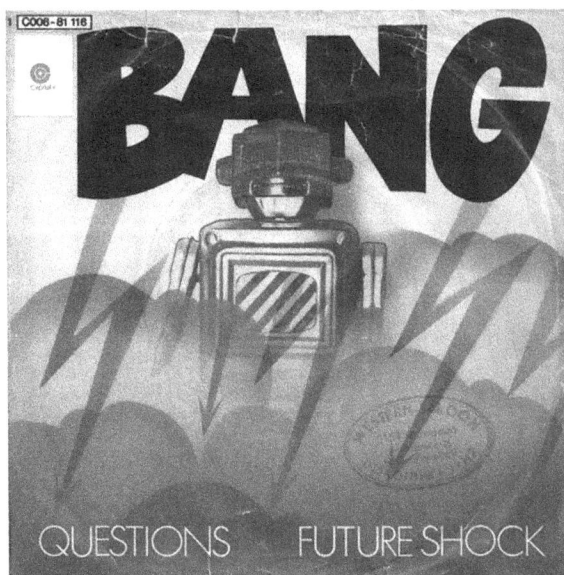

BANG on the Capitol roof for "BANGday", June 7, 1972.

After the show in Dallas, Texas.

Frank rehearsing at the Sportatorium in Hollywood, Florida.

After the show in Birmingham, Alabama.

Frankie onstage.

Tommy Wingate.

Frankie at the Mar y Sol fest in Puerto Rico, April 2, 1972.

Frank and Frankie onstage in North Carolina.

Tony onstage.

Stage at Mar y Sol in Puerto Rico.

Frank working the crowd at Rock Spectacular.

Frank and Frankie onstage.

CHAPTER 5

Mother/Bow to the King

AT THIS TIME there were personnel changes within Capitol's hierarchy including vice president Herb Belkin, who went to the A&R division, and producer Michael Sunday, who left to take up a better offer from Epic Records. He asked BANG to follow him but the band had signed a four-album deal with Capitol, who refused to let them go. Instead, the label placed BANG with producer Jeffrey Cheen, who had previously been with Tetragrammaton and Mercury Records with the new president of Capitol, Artie Mogull, before moving over to Capitol's A&R department, where he also worked with legendary Hollywood hustler Kim Fowley on his *International Heroes* album.

Said Herb Belkin in a 1998 interview with Robert Silverstein, "I joined Capitol Records in late 1969 and I went to work for them on the East Coast. Around that time, EMI acquired the company. Then, in early-mid '70, they discovered that Capitol, for the first time in it's history, was going to lose money. And so, they started this huge shake up. Since I was a lawyer hired from the West Coast, every time they fired someone they'd give me his job. So literally I'm in the music business maybe six months and I became the head of East Coast operations for Capitol Records. I get to the point where they let everybody go and I'm sitting in my office on 6th Avenue one day and the phone rings. A disconnected voice on the other end says to me, 'Belkin, A&R is like baseball, you get three strikes and you're out, start swinging.' About 10 days later, a guy by the name of Artie Mogull, who was the head of A&R for Capitol comes to New York and says to me, "So what'ya got for me?" So from that point on, I started crawling at the clubs, talking to people and finding things and I signed a couple artists. About a year later, they invited me out to California and become the head of the A&R department. In the '60s and '70s the business was so crazy and frenetic, things like that happened all the time. There were a lot of interesting bands that came out from that time. It was a circus, the whole business was a circus in those days."

TONY, FRANK, AND Frankie went about writing some songs when they were back in Fort Lauderdale at the Escape. These songs would become the *Mother/Bow to the King* album. They rehearsed them at the Sportatorium, during the day, while it was empty.

"It was really cool," recalled Frank, "to create and practice those songs in such a big auditorium. The sound was amazing."

While the band was jamming, Steve and Danny, the roadies, would walk through the stadium, which hadn't been cleaned from the prior night's activities and find money, drugs, and other stuff. Said Frank, "It's amazing what people lose when they're stoned and partying."

In late May and early June the band started recording the *Mother/Bow to the King* album at Criteria Studios with Jeff Cheen as producer and Karl Richardson as engineer. Early on, it was evident to Jeff that the drums required more polish. His focus was on Tony. He suggested a change of venue in order to coincide with the upcoming BANG Day at Capitol and arranged for the recording to transition to The Sound Factory in Los Angeles. David Hassinger would take over the engineering there and John Palladino partnered as a co-producer.

DAVID HASSINGER PURCHASED Moonglow Records and the Moonglow recording studio on Selma Avenue, in Hollywood, California, in 1969. He changed the name to The Sound Factory and opened his doors to some of the bigger acts of the era, including Gram Parsons, Ringo Starr, Dolly Parton, Brian Wilson, the Jackson Five, and many more. BANG arrived on Monday, June 5, 1972, to continue work on what would become the *Mother/Bow to the King* album.

"Top engineer, top place—the best," enthused Tony.

"Capitol wanted us to record in the Capitol studios," said Jeff Cheen. "Nobody got Hassinger in those days—he was recording the Rolling Stones and in great demand. We were able to get him."

"In this same studio, 'Incense and Peppermints' by the Strawberry Alarm Clock was recorded," said Frank. "Frankie Valli had just finished recording 'My Eyes Adored You.' While we were waiting to start our session, Seals and Crofts were finishing production on 'Diamond Girl.'"

WEDNESDAY, JUNE 7, was a very special day for the band. One of the label's most memorable promotional stunts was to declare "BANG Day" at Capitol Records, although this nearly went ahead without the band's participation, as Tony explained, "It's about three AM, the morning of BANG Day in Hollywood. Frank and I are walking the strip, heading back to the hotel after exploring Hollywood Boulevard. At the time, longhairs were viewed with suspicion, especially by the authorities. Being in the middle of the block, we casually crossed the street, like we would in Claymont or Philly. There was no traffic and few, if any, people. Suddenly, police were yelling at us. 'Stop, put up your hands, don't move!' They cuffed us roughly and drove us to jail. Here we were, a few hours from BANG Day and we're sitting in jail for jaywalking. Eventually, we got in touch with our manager, Rick, who bailed us out in time for the party.

"Not having slept yet, we entered the Capitol Tower building later that morning, where we were met with BANG posters, balloons, album covers, guns, and explosions. In the elevators, BANG music was playing. I still remember riding up to the offices of the 'big guys' in their expensive suits listening to 'Future Shock' as background music.

"Things were strange and exciting—our management hired a helicopter to fly around Los Angeles and the Capitol Tower, dragging a sign that read, 'Capitol BANG loves you!' After posing for promo pictures and such, we made our way to the party on a lower floor. For some reason, the promotion department associated our name BANG with sex, so when we walked into the big party room, they were showing porno movies made in the 1920s, something like *Debbie Does The Keystone Cops*. At the time, it was all a little embarrassing but it was our day and everybody loved us. Hello rock and roll!

"I'd like to say we were totally humbled by our good fortune and to a point, we were. But we had worked long and hard preparing for this time. The high from BANG Day gave us a confidence and swagger. We knew we were good and had what it took to make it. Later that week, when we went to court, we brought some BANG albums and promo stuff for the judge and cops. Everyone was happy. They still fined us."

Meanwhile, Frank explained what was happening behind the scenes, "What was happening at Capitol was that everybody was fired who were working in some way with BANG and a whole new group of people came in who had their own bands that they were trying to push. It was like, 'Hey, I have my band, why do I wanna push BANG?'"

At the moment when BANG should have been on top of the world, the rug was pulled from underneath them.

Tony continued, "So we go out to California to record. We come to the studio the next day (June 8th) and there's some guy sitting in the drum booth. It's Bruce Gary (subsequently with The Knack)—I mean, one of the best rock drummers around! I'm suddenly not playing on the album?"

"Producer Cheen decided that Tony wasn't going to play," explained Frank, regarding the basic track for "Keep On" they were working on that day.

"I wasn't happy with the drum parts I was hearing from Tony and I knew Bruce was the way to go," recalled Jeff Cheen.

Frank and Frankie appealed to Rick Bowen, their manager but Rick was completely on board with the change of drummer. "Get with the program, man," said Rick to the Franks, "or I won't be managing you anymore."

Tony continued, "I'm crushed; Frank and Frankie are wide-eyed! Here we are going from a basement in Claymont, Delaware, to having BANG Day at Capitol Records and now this. All this incredible stuff was happening and suddenly the three of us—the marriage, I mean someone's coming in between us. This happened to so many bands. Some asshole screwed things up. So, I said, 'Fine, I'll go along. And in the meantime, I'll practice more so I can get better for the next album, the next whatever. I'll play on it.' I started playing drums when I was 25 until, four years later, when Bruce retired me. Watching this guy play, wow, he was so good, incredible. If there's anyone to replace me, it's Bruce."

AROUND THIS TIME, while in Los Angeles, the band had an off-day. Frank and Frankie headed to see the recently-released pornographic film *Deep Throat*. After being in the studio, they were famished. Before going into the movie, they stopped at the concession stand and purchased hot dogs. As they entered the theater, the movie was under way, just at the scene where Linda Lovelace was going down on the doctor. They walked in with their hot dogs in hand to discover dozens of patrons staring at them and laughing. The guys quickly dumped the dogs in the trash, completely embarrassed.

THE BAND APPEARED with Edgar Winter for a concert in Birmingham, Alabama, on June 14, 1972 and then joined Three Dog Night on tour, for a six date swing through the South. This collaboration began on Friday, June 30, in Jacksonville, Florida. The next night, the groups headed south to Tampa Stadium, in Tampa, Florida, joining with Frampton-less Humble Pie. A Miami appearance on July 2nd followed.

Recalled Frank, "The biggest, best concert we played was at Tampa Stadium (July 1, 1972). The stage was set in the end zone—Three Dog Night and Humble Pie—people were in seats on left and right—BANG was to open. Tony's idea was to start at the other end zone and walk up the middle of the football field. People went nuts because they knew the concert was going to start. We played 'Questions'—the whole stadium was rocking back and forth. There was a delay because of the sound. Watching the crowd was throwing him off, so he couldn't watch it."

On July 2nd, the band was at the Sportatorium in Miami to open for Three Dog Night and Buddy Miles. As the bands were getting ready in their respective trailers, there was a loud knock at BANG's door. Someone was pounding on it. Frank opened it to discover Buddy Miles, totally losing his temper.

"Where's Chuck from Three Dog?" he demanded. "Gimme Chuck from Three Dog."

Buddy was at the wrong trailer and was upset about some bad drugs provided to him by Chuck Negron, from Three Dog Night. After Frank and Frankie, horrified, pointed next door,

Buddy moved on to the next trailer and threatened Chuck with a gun. Apparently everything was settled, somehow, because everyone played that night and was alive the next morning.

AFTER A BREAK to attend Rick Bowen's wedding in Savannah, Georgia, on Independence Day, July 4th, the band enjoyed some time at home, playing a gig at the Anvil Inn in Kennett Square, Pennsylvania, on the 5th. Three days later, guitarist Frankie Gilcken got married.

The band rejoined Three Dog Night for three more appearances—two in Orlando, Florida, on July 20th and 21st and one in Charlotte, North Carolina, on July 23rd. Three Dog Night was riding high, with a #1 single, "Black and White," from their recently released blockbuster album *Seven Separate Fools*. The prior year, the band had soared to the top of the charts with "Old Fashioned Love Song" and "Never Been to Spain," following 1970's "Joy to the World." These were the last shows with Tony as the drummer.

THE BAND WAS back in Miami, Florida, at Criteria Studios, to record "Humble" on July 26th. Tony had written the lyrics while on the frightening DC3 flight to Puerto Rico. But, the drummer controversy was proving too tense for him. "So then we get into a thing—the band—the three of us—this whole thing separating the Franks and me. The bond we had—brothers on a quest together. I left the group. I said, 'I'm gone.' And I went back home to Claymont. The Franks finished up the album. We'd already written all the songs. We had been in Criteria and recorded a bunch of the songs. The producer took them back into the studio and brought in Duris Maxwell, of Skylark, to record over all the stuff that I had done for the *Mother/Bow To The King* album. The only thing of me remaining is the backwards highhat on 'Humble.' And I was back up in Delaware in the retail business, selling white socks, wondering how my life had gone down the tubes. At the same time, this was affecting my wife and kids. I remembered them watching me play at the Sportatorum, in Hollywood, Florida, standing off stage. They were little kids, wondering 'What's daddy doing?'

TONY DIORIO LEFT the band on July 30, 1972. The following day, the Franks picked up the pieces and continued work on

"Feel the Hurt" and "Bow to the King." The band finished mixing the songs by August 10, in time to meet up with Ted Nugent and the Amboy Dukes for two dates in Tennessee; August 11th in Chattanooga and the 13th in Memphis. They also played with Three Dog Night in Birmingham, Alabama on the 12th. Duris Maxwell, of Skylark, played drums at these concerts. Skylark was also managed by Rick Bowen and was staying at the Escape Hotel.

"This was the time we had another harrowing flight," recalled Frank. "We were flying from Memphis back to Fort Lauderdale. As we were about to land, the pilot suddenly pulled up at the last minute, aborting the landing. We then began circling the Everglades. After about ten minutes, the pilot informed us the front landing gear was stuck and we needed to do an emergency landing at nearby Homestead Air Force Base. The next thing we knew, we were being told to brace! The cabin door was open and we were sitting near the cockpit. We could see one pilot at the wheel while the co-pilot was pushing hard on the brake. The runway was sprayed full of foam, as we were coming down. There were emergency trucks all around us. The pilots had to keep the nose up and stop the plane at the same time. Miraculously, they did it. It was actually a very smooth landing under the circumstances. No one was injured and the press mobbed us as we came off the plane. We gave an interview to a television reporter. It was all very surreal."

THE FRANKS RETURNED to Philadelphia on the 15th for a break and looked to add band members.

Tony recalled, "When the Franks came back, they'd got the acetate of the album and I was in tears listening to this thing, it sounded so good, hearing all the songs finished. They dedicated the album to me and all that kind of crap. I was still tight with the Franks, even though I was initially very pissed. They didn't know what to do. They were teenagers, just a couple of kids. I was already married, had kids and could appreciate what was happening to us because I had already had a gig. I mean, I had the day job. So to me, this was incredible. This was a dream come true. To them, it was just part of life. 'Okay, I'm seventeen, now I'm a rock star.'"

"So many things happened to the group in that six-month period between the *BANG* album and *Mother/Bow To The King*," admitted Frank. "We lost Tony as our drummer and also our producer, Michael Sunday, went to Epic Records. Our second producer didn't have the same vision for us that Michael had. With Tony gone, we used session drummers Bruce Gary and Duris Maxwell. They did a great job, though."

DURING THIS BREAK, the album cover for *Mother/Bow to the King* was shot at the Brandywine Battlefield in Chadds Ford, Pennsylvania, near Philadelphia. Gary Osier, photographed wearing a cape, was on the cover, even though he did not play on the record.

Mike "Mace" Maben and Gary Osier officially joined the band on the 22nd. Mace and Gary would later go on to found the popular band Texas, that nearly broke through in the 70s and included Frankie Gilcken in the lineup.

The following day, Wednesday, August 23, 1972, BANG was at Idora Park in Youngstown, Ohio, for a concert with the Eagles and The Doobie Brothers. *Eagles*, the debut album for the Glenn Frey, Don Henley, et al, ensemble had been released in June, featuring the hit "Take It Easy." The Doobies had premiered in 1971 but were now having commercial success with their second album, *Toulouse Street*, which had been released the prior month and had two hits receiving airplay: "Listen to the Music" and "Jesus Is Just Alright."

Earlier in the summer, Hurricane Agnes had hung over the east coast of the USA for nine days in June, causing billions of dollars of damage, mostly from flooding. On August 25th, BANG played at a Hurricane Agnes benefit concert at the amusement park at Williams Grove, Pennsylvania, just south of Mechanicsburg. Bob Seger also appeared at this concert, which was broadcast by the public television station out of York, Pennsylvania. According to the local papers, only 350 showed up of 800 expected, putting the promoter, Roach Productions, in the hole. This poor turnout discouraged Capitol from funding a larger benefit for Agnes.

The boys joined Seger, who had yet to follow up his top 20 hit "Ramblin' Gamblin' Man" from 1969, for another date in Thomasville, North Carolina, the following night. Four albums later, Seger had a few minor hits and was a few years away from his mega-hit *Night Moves*.

After stops in Pittsburgh, Pennsylvania, with Ted Nugent on the 27th and in Detroit, Michigan, with Mitch Ryder the following night, the boys headed south for two performances in Louisiana with Brownsville Station: August 30th in Baton Rouge and August 31st in Lake Charles. Brownsville Station, now two records into their careers, had also experienced modest album sales to date, similar to BANG and were a year away from their hit "Smokin' in the Boy's Room."

The next stop was Port Arthur, Texas, on Saturday, September 2, 1972, with Bob Seger. As the concert was ending, the promoter threatened not to pay either band because the total performance was ten minutes short. So, Seger and BANG got together on stage and performed "Gimme Some Lovin'", to the crowd's delight. All the performers were then paid.

BANG WAS NEXT off to the Erie Canal "Soda" Pop Festival scheduled for Labor Day weekend, September 2nd through the 4th, near Griffin, Indiana. Approximately a quarter million people attended this affair, which was plagued by a shortage of food and drink and a good deal of anarchy. The crowd was nearly four times what the promoters expected and they quickly lost control. Roads had been backed up for twenty miles, as the weekend was beginning.

According to the Associated Press, the Indiana State Police described the roads as "wall to wall hippies." Lt. Norman Burnsworth, commander of the Evansville State Police post, said, "Traffic trying to reach the rock festival on Bull Island resulted in the closure of Interstate 64, from Grayville, Illinois, to U.S. 41, about 25 miles north of Evansville. It must be the biggest crowd that ever turned out for anything in Indiana, besides the Indianapolis 500."

The festival was actually held in Illinois, however, keeping the Indiana State Police at bay. Bull Island was connected by land to Indiana but had the Wabash River to its south and west, providing a water barrier to the rest of Illinois. The Illinois State Police stayed away because there was no over-land access to the island from their side.

The *Indianapolis Star* headlined on September 2, "Quarter Million Young People Take 'Trip' to Soda Pop Festival: Drugs, Drink, Mark Rock Blast: Police Do Not Interfere With Pot,

Alcohol Users At Giant Festival." According to staff reporter Joseph Gelarden, a police official told him, "The situation is hopeless." There were concerns the crowd could reach a half million. National Guardsmen were ready.

Gelarden continued, "As the raucous sounds of rock band music slammed across a broad meadow on the tree-lined peninsula, hundreds of youths openly smoked marijuana and drank beer and wine. Some of the drug-sickened youths had injected directly into their bloodstreams bleach crystals they had purchased at the festival site in the belief they were amphetamines. Medical personnel were treating youths suffering drug overdoses on the average of one every five minutes. A man, about 30, stood on the platform for several hours warning fans that the 'green and blue acid is bad—but the sugar cubes are good.'"

As the weekend continued, thousands abandoned their cars along Interstate 64 and walked up to ten miles to the concert site. Attendance surpassed 300,000 by Labor Day, Monday, according to some estimates.

Flash Cadillac & the Continental Kids, Black Oak Arkansas, Ramatam, Mike Quatro, BANG, Cheech and Chong, Foghat, Albert King, Brownsville Station, Santana, Canned Heat, Flash, Ravi Shankar, Rory Gallagher, Lee Michaels and Frosty, Eagles, The Amboy Dukes, Farm, CK Thunder, and Gentle Giant performed over the three days. Black Sabbath, Fleetwood Mac, Nazareth, Allman Brothers, and several other bands on the original bill were unable to, or chose not to make it due to financial disputes. The absence of most of the headliners upset the crowd.

The final day of the festival, Faces, Fleetwood Mac, Ball and Jack, The Doors, Boone's Farm, Fluorescent Leech and Eddie, Eagles, BANG, Doobie Brothers, Nazareth, and Danny O'Keefe were scheduled, though not all played. As BANG was setting up, they could not find the promoter to receive their final installment. They were the last to play and as the festival ended, the remnants of the crowd burned the stage. BANG had to quickly remove their equipment and run for their lives! The problem was, they had no money and had to get home.

Back at the hotel, they phoned Rick Bowen, their manager, to explain the situation and get some cash.

"I'm a married man now," scolded Bowen, "don't ever call me after 11 again!"

The Doobie Brothers, who were staying at the same hotel and had also been stiffed by the promoter, became aware of BANG's predicament and without being asked, offered them $500 to get them home. BANG, to this day, remains grateful to the Doobie Brothers for this unselfish act of kindness.

David Berry, a reporter for the Evansville, Indiana, *Courier*, described the subsequent exodus from the festival as like a "never-ending line of refugees from a war-torn country . . . carrying tents, sleeping bags and coolers."

Sgt. Don Lehr of the Indiana State Police described the scene left behind the next day as "a gigantic garbage pile."

Remaining were tons of trash, makeshift shelters, panties and smells of campfires, burning garbage, marijuana, and human waste.

AFTER A MONTH hiatus to practice with their new members, BANG was back on the road on October 7, 1972, appearing with MC5 in Detroit, Michigan. That Monday, October 9, the *Mother/Bow to the King* album (Capitol Records, SMAS-11110) was released.

Right from the rural, acoustic-based beginning of the opening track "Mother," BANG's second album for Capitol widened their artistic horizons. Tracks like "Keep On" (Capitol Records, 3386), issued as a single just prior to the album's release, "Idealist...Realist" and the guitar-fest "Humble" were straight-ahead, balls-to-the-wall, metallic rockers and pretty much business as usual. But, in general, *Mother/Bow To The King* boasted plenty of light and shade. "Feel The Hurt" hinted at the radio-friendly classic rock sound of bands like Lynyrd Skynyrd, while "Tomorrow" and the mellow, melodic and utterly magnificent "Bow To The King"—featuring some highly effective Mellotron—occupied the same early 70s progressive rock territory as Wishbone Ash or even early Genesis.

And then there was "No Sugar Tonight" (Capitol Records, 3474). Penned by Randy Bachman, the song had been the B-side of the Guess Who's "American Woman," which had topped the US singles chart a couple of years earlier. Recorded because, in Frank's words, "Capitol were trying their best to make us a commercial band," BANG disliked "No Sugar Tonight" so much that, when they made *Mother/Bow To The King* available via their website a few years ago, they excised it from the album. Nevertheless, the track clearly had commercial potential and it was released as a single. Like its predecessor, *Mother/Bow To The King* was favorably received by the critics. *Billboard* listed it in the "Special Merit Picks" section, claiming that the album "features strong, commercial rock which should receive both AM and FM play. Frank Ferrara shows strong vocals throughout and Frank Gilcken complements this with his guitar. Strong treatment of the old Guess Who rocker 'No Sugar Tonight,' which is getting some radio action . . ."

"The song 'Bow to the King' was written about Muhammad Ali," said Tony, "who we were privileged to meet one day in the Philadelphia airport. We told him about the album and that we had mailed him a copy after it's release. Ali told us he would look for it when he got home, where he was headed. Later that night I answered the phone to 'this is Mrs. Muhammad Ali, we found the album and my husband says he will listen to it tonight.' Days later, we received an autographed picture with a note saying 'The next time I fight Joe Frazier, he will Bow to the King.' What we remember most is how 'The Greatest' had the softest hand shake you could imagine."

TUESDAY, OCTOBER 17, the band was in Atlanta, Georgia, with Steve Miller Band, who were beginning to move away from their psychedelic roots. *The Joker* was still a year away but the band was beginning a change over to a more commercial sound. Before playing the show, Frank and Frankie went to The Underground to go shopping and found six-inch platform shoes. The stage was poorly made of plywood, with a lot of soft spots and the guys had a lot of trouble with the new shoes but they made them part of their attire going forward.

This same day, attorney William Krasilovsky sent a letter to Rick Bowen, describing the terms of a possible settlement regarding Tony Diorio's termination. The legal wrangling with Bowen was just beginning for the band.

BANG FOLLOWED UP with appearances in Winston-Salem, North Carolina, on October 20, Montgomery, Alabama, on the 21st and Hazelton, Pennsylvania on the 26th.

On Friday, the 27th, BANG was in Syracuse, New York. During the performance, Frank jumped down into the audience.

When he went to jump back on stage, he didn't quite make it in his platform shoes and split his satin pants completely, from back to front.

"I laid on the stage covering my **JUNK** with my bass," remembered Frank, "until the club owner brought me his raincoat to cover me. Too bad Spandex hadn't been invented yet! After the show, we joked that me splitting my pants was the highlight of the set and that we should make it part of the show. That never happened."

Saturday, the 28th, the band was in Baltimore for an appearance on the *Barry Richards Show*.

EARLY NOVEMBER, WHILE the Nixon vs. McGovern presidential election was under way, the band toured the Midwest, with stops in Grand Rapids, Michigan on the 4th, Cleveland, Ohio, on the 6th, Toledo, Ohio on Election Day, the 7th, Columbus, Ohio, on the 9th, and Detroit, Michigan, on the 11th. For the Ohio dates, the band played with Trapeze at the Agora, which was a club in all three cities. Around this time, Rick Bowen had sent a contract to attempt to renew their relationship for another year but it went unsigned.

BANG THEN SWUNG south for four dates in Texas: Beaumont on the 15th, Amarillo on the 17th, San Antonio on the 19th, and Dallas on the 20th.

On November 23rd, the band did the Gatlin Creek Festival in Gatlin Creek, Texas. The next day, they were off to Charlotte, North Carolina.

Meanwhile, back in the Miami, Florida, area, Rick Bowen's Elton John concert at the Sportatorium was patrolled by 35 security personnel and was being closely watched by the sheriff. A local judge had ordered this to be the last concert at the venue until all reported fire, building, and health code violations were addressed and an occupancy permit issued. The crowd was limited to only 8,800 patrons for this show and no more than 6,000 for future shows. The promoters also had to search patrons for drugs and alcohol as they entered.

Additional BANG shows through the end of the year included:
December 7th – Mount Pleasant, Michigan
December 10th – Hazelton, Pennsylvania

December 11th – Altoona, Pennsylvania
December 12th – Akron, Ohio
December 13th – Ada, Oklahoma
December 15th – Louisville, Kentucky
December 27th – Duluth, Minnesota
December 28th – Minneapolis, Minnesota
December 30th – Augusta, Georgia
December 31th – Miami, Florida

For each of these shows, the band was the headliner but drove long distances, often overnight. The last show, in Miami, was with Black Oak Arkansas at Pirate's World. It would be the last show with Rick Bowen as manager and Mace Maben and Gary Osier as band members.

Attorney Krasilovsky had sent a confidential letter to Herb Belkin of Capitol Records, early in December, suggesting that the contract with Rick Bowen was invalid due to the Franks being minors. He sought Herb's opinion of Capitol's position in the matter and suggested BANG could have a direct relationship with the label, rather than working through Bowen.

The attorney and the band did not know, at the time, that Belkin was shortly on his way to Atlantic Records. Said Herb, in 1998, "When I left Capitol in 1972, I was courted by Jerry Greenberg and Jerry Wexler at Atlantic, at that time, to take over and run the West Coast operation of Atlantic Records—which I did for about a year and a half. I developed a lot of their marketing plans including a whole program, which we called 'The British Invasion' or 'The Rockers From Britain.' It started with Led Zeppelin and then Yes, King Crimson, ELP, and Roxy Music. Also, about that time, we broke Dr. John. It was very cool. The result of that was about a year after I got there, they asked me to come back to New York and become the head of marketing for Atlantic Records." Herb did not think to take BANG along with him to Atlantic.

After the Akron show on the 12th, the Franks wrote a letter to Rick Bowen complaining about the lack of attention and their inability to subsist on the road, due to infrequent and inadequate payments. Said the letter:

". . . Rick, one year ago, you were the answer to our dreams. You were the guiding light for three very scared people . . . now, when we need you the most and you should be helping us more, you are helping us less than ever before."

A WEEK LATER, on the 20th, Tony Diorio absolved all claims on Rick Bowen for his termination in consideration of one dollar. Tony was trying to shake himself free of Rick in time for the Franks to send Bowen a termination letter the day after Christmas.

ON DECEMBER 31, 1972, baseball star Roberto Clemente was killed in a plane crash, as the DC7 he was on crashed after take-off near San Juan, Puerto Rico.

...

"Tomorrow may be a beautiful day
Tomorrow may bring a much better way
To find your place and what you must do
To face all the problems that are facing you"

—Lyrics from *Tomorrow*

Attention! Attention!
Announcing: Bang Day !!!!
Wednesday, June 7, 1972

As part of our ever-increasing efforts to introduce our new up-and-coming artists to the Capitol Tower, we take great pleasure in announcing Bang Day!

As part of the day's activities, you are all cordially invited to a "vino" cocktail party on Wednesday afternoon at 5:30 on the 12th floor, where you will have the opportunity to meet the members of Bang. (if you can "rip-off" a Bang T-shirt, be sure to wear it on Wednesday!)

Rock 'n' roll !!!
© in DINO AIRALI

A & R Dept.

BANG Day invitation.

Soda Pop Festival ticket.

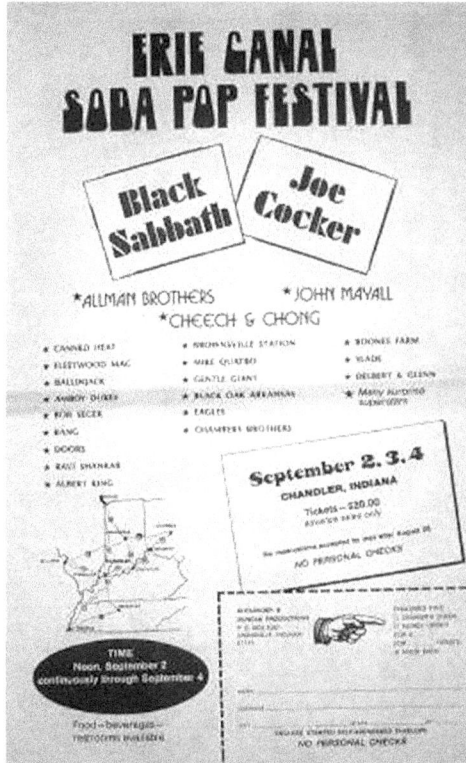

Soda Pop Festival poster.

BANG with Jeff Cheen outside Capitol Records in Hollywood, California, on June 7, 1972.

Steve Hiner, Frank Ferrara, Timmy Trainor, and Frankie Gilcken.

Inside cover of the *Mother* album.

Frankie with Gary Osier and Mace Maben at the Atlanta airport.

In Rick Bowen's office. Standing: BANG with Rick Bowen and
Jimmy Ienner. Seated: Herb Belkin.

Christmas in 1972 with Mace and Gary.

Frank without his Stash while in Minnesota.

Outtake for *Mother* album cover shoot.

Mother/Bow to the King album cover.

Timmy and Steve loading the truck.

Bright Lights

Tony being told he's being replaced with Bruce Gary at the Sound Factory in Hollywood, California, by co-producer John Palladino (seated) and Jeff Cheen.

Frankie and Frank helping Tony move to Florida.

Poster for the BANGshow with Trapeze at the Agora in Ohio,
November 1972.

CHAPTER 6

MUSIC

THE NEW YEAR began with more legal battles. On the 17th the attorney announced to Capitol Records the termination of Rick Bowen as manager. The letter expressed the band's desire to continue with Capitol directly.

But, it was hard to shake Rick Bowen off of them. The following week Rick told Frankie in a letter that he would never terminate the contract. He reminded the band how much he had invested in them and groused about $900 in phone calls charged to his American Express. He warned the band to stop using his card.

Simultaneously, Diversified Management Associates, who had been booking shows outside of the reach of Concerts West and East Coast Concerts, demanded a three month extension to their contract, which also involved Rick Bowen, due to the band taking a three-month hiatus the prior year.

Heated exchanges continued between Bowen and the attorney and others, to which Bowen was warned against potential libel and defamation.

Also this January, Bowen had decided to leave East Coast Concerts and work directly for Concerts West out of Dallas, Texas. Rick and other promoters in the greater-Miami area were complaining about the venues and their capacity. "For the most popular groups," said one promoter, "we need 6,000 people to break even . . . there is a large audience for rock and pop concerts here . . . but they won't go to the Sportatorium or to Pirate's World because of the conditions at those places."

AFTER CANCELING AN appearance with Brownsville Station and Cactus at the Rockford Armory, in Rockford, Illinois, on January 27, 1973, to benefit the Rockford Boys Club, the band was off the road and settling in for some writing.

In February, 1973, they wrote and recorded "Glad You're Home" at Virtue Studios in Philadelphia. Tony Orlando and Dawn's "Tie a Yellow Ribbon" was tearing up the charts and Tony Diorio thought a song about Vietnam veterans would do well, so he took the rough cut to CAM, their publisher, in New York, where it was well-received. On the 20th of February, the band finished mixing the song at Virtue. The next day, they learned from Jeff Cheen that Capitol refused to release any singles involving POWs, not wanting the band to be pigeon-holed. The band was told to save the song for their next album.

On February 23rd Bob Johnson and Denny D'Agostino joined the band. Despite the difficulties with management, the band remained optimistic about their future. Former drummer Tony Diorio now took over the reins as manager and the guys formed FTF Enterprises.

Said Tony, "We got guitarists and drummers to fill in with the band and I went to Capitol to negotiate a third album, *Music*. We also had renegotiated our publishing deal. I was managing and things were looking good . . ."

Soon after Tony's visit to Los Angeles on March 5, 1973, the band spent the month working on the *Music* album at the Sound Factory. After practicing at Emitt Rhodes Studio with Bruce Gary on the 13th, the band recorded "Must Be Love," "Page of My Life," "Another Town," "Love Sonnet," and "Brightness" on the 19th, and "Need Nobody," "Windfair," "Little Boy Blue," "Glad You're Home," "Pearl and Her Ladies," and "Exactly Who I Am" the next day. Tony won an audition for finger-snaps to include on this last track. The next two weeks were spent adding overdubs and mixing. The band then began rehearsing with the new members.

Frank added, "By the time the *Music* album came out, our label support was almost nil. Everyone at Capitol that believed in BANG was gone. We recorded the *Music* album in Los Angeles, at the Sound Factory, with Dave Hassinger. Again, Bruce played drums and did a great job. I love the drum tracks on the *Music* album. Every album was unique in its own way but the *Music* album was probably my favorite."

MUSIC   109

Frank's comment that *Music* is probably his favorite BANG album is interesting, because it bears little or no resemblance to the band's previous work. Notwithstanding a couple of tracks (namely "Don't Need Nobody" and "Exactly Who I Am") in which guitarist Frankie seemed to hanker for days of yore, *Music* was a compendium of tight, radio-friendly, three-minute pop songs, with jangling guitars and occasional piano/Mellotron fills matched to hook-laden melodies. Moreover, Frank's vocals had lost the wailing Ozzy/Plant inflections, to be replaced by an understated, more wistful approach.

Indeed, *Music* could be considered the great lost early 70s power-pop album, operating in the same field as the likes of Big Star, Blue Ash, and even the Raspberries, who contributed backing vocals to the careening "Must Be Love." Despite a couple of misfires, the album is an attractive, cohesive work, with highlights including "Glad You're Home" (the song about returning Vietnam POWs), the irresistible "Page Of My Life," "Little Boy Blue," and a fabulously witty vignette about groupies, "Pearl And Her Ladies."

Frankie Gilcken explained, there was a reason for the sudden shift in BANG's sound. "We'd just signed a deal with a publishing company that was run by Raspberries producer Jimmy Ienner. Both Jimmy and Capitol said that they wanted us to go in a similar direction to the Raspberries, which is why *Music* sounded the way it did. It was a chance for us to do something different but even so, it wasn't really what BANG was about."

A success on its own terms, *Music* must nevertheless have been something of a shock to the band's fan-base. "I love heavy metal but I also love other things too," said Tony. "By the time we got to the *Music* album, we thought that we probably lost part of our edge and got too light. Our musical tastes were expanding. We were just going through what every band goes through. We didn't say, 'We need a heavy tune.' We started writing a tune and it was whatever it was. We just took it wherever it went."

BANG suddenly came up against a brick wall. *Music* and the single "Must Be Love" failed to make a mark and they suddenly found gigs hard to come by. The reason for this would take a while to reach the band but meanwhile, Capitol's idea of a solution was to implore BANG to become just another pop group.

"Capitol actually came to us and asked us to write a song like 'I Am Woman' by Helen Reddy, because that was a hit," laughed Tony. "They said we needed to write a song like 'I Am Woman.' Are you kidding?

BACK AT HOME in Philadelphia, CAM and the attorney helped finalize the release and settlement with Rick Bowen. At this time, the new entity FTF Enterprises, representing Frankie, Tony, and Frank, began pitching management agencies. The David Forest Agency, on the west coast, was first but it was to no avail.

The band prepared for another concert tour to promote their new album. First up was Knoxville, Tennessee, on May 4th. This was followed by dates in Hamlet, North Carolina, on the 6th, Space Lab, Florida, on the 14th, and Orlando, Florida, on the 19th. "Must Be Love" (Capitol Records, 3622) and the *Music* album (Capitol Records, ST-11190) were released on Monday, May 21st, 1973.

THE BAND WAS back at Fort Bragg, North Carolina, on May 24th, to participate in the second *Harmony Through Music*. The Soul Serenadors, Demitriss Trapp, The Platters, Bill Deal and the Rhondels, and Leroy Van Dyke also performed. According to Terry McBryde, reporter for the *Fayetteville Observer*, "The highlight came when the rock group BANG appeared. Teenagers were trying to crawl under the fence separating them from the performers. The group left the stage finally with cheers of 'We want BANG!' lingering for several minutes."

NEXT, THEY WERE on to Charlotte, North Carolina, on the 25th, Fort Worth, Texas, on June 7th, Montgomery, Alabama on June 8th, and Chattanooga, Tennessee, on the 10th, before dropping by Atlantic City, New Jersey, on June 30th to appear on the television program *Summertime on the Pier* with Ed Hurst.

FTF next tried to sign up with the International Agency for a management deal. The agency was concerned the band was still under contract with Rick Bowen and DMA. Despite assurances from the attorney that all was settled and there was no contractual relationship anymore, the agency didn't bite.

FTF also expressed their frustrations to the Capitol Records marketing department when they discovered BANG had been excluded from their current marketing catalog despite just releasing a new album. Quietly, they sent an exploratory letter to Polydor Records, contemplating a label switch.

NEAR THE END of July, on the 26th, the band was in Meridian, Mississippi, for a concert, before returning to Pennypack Park, at Rhawn and Winchester Avenues, in Philadelphia, Pennsylvania, for a show on July 30th. That event was a free concert as part of the Pennypack Park Festival that also included Ten Wheel Drive, an American jazz-rock band, and Forest Green, Capitol recording artists. Because the venue was so close to home, Frank brought his parents along. His mother looked upon him lovingly while he sang 'Mother,' not realizing it was not a love song dedicated to her.

Then, it was back south again, for appearances in Valdosta, Georgia, on August 3rd, Columbus, Mississippi, on the 4th, and St. Louis, Missouri, on the 9th, with Bachman Turner Overdrive. Apparently, the touring schedule was getting to Bob Johnson, who quit the band on the 16th. Carl Bachman, not related to the BTO Bachmans, then came on board on the 28th.

AROUND THIS TIME, the band was informed that Capitol Records did not intend to invest in another album with the band but instead offered recording some singles in Los Angeles. FTF sent a request for funds to cover their travel and lodging expenses. Capitol obliged.

THE BAND SPENT the week around Labor Day rehearsing, before heading off to Fayetteville, North Carolina, for an appearance on September 5th. They followed this up with a concert in Fort Smith, Arkansas, on the 8th, with the Lee Pickens Group and another show on the 10th. Pickens was formerly of Bloodrock.

...

**"Should I think about my sorrow
That I know I cannot change
So distant seems my happiness
So real is my pain"**

—Lyrics from *Feel the Hurt*

BTO concert marquis.

Bruce Gary on the roof at Capitol.

At the Sound Factory recording with Dave Hassinger (behind the board) and Jeff Cheen (standing on the right).

BANG at the Sound Factory recording the MUSIC album, March 1973.

Frank doing vocals for the MUSIC album at the Sound Factory.

Frankie during MUSIC sessions at the Sound Factory.

In the lobby of the Sound Factory with Bruce Gary and Dave Hassinger (seated).

Bruce Gary in studio with Tim Trainor (left).

Tony at the board during MUSIC sessions.

Frank at the piano during the recording of the MUSIC album.

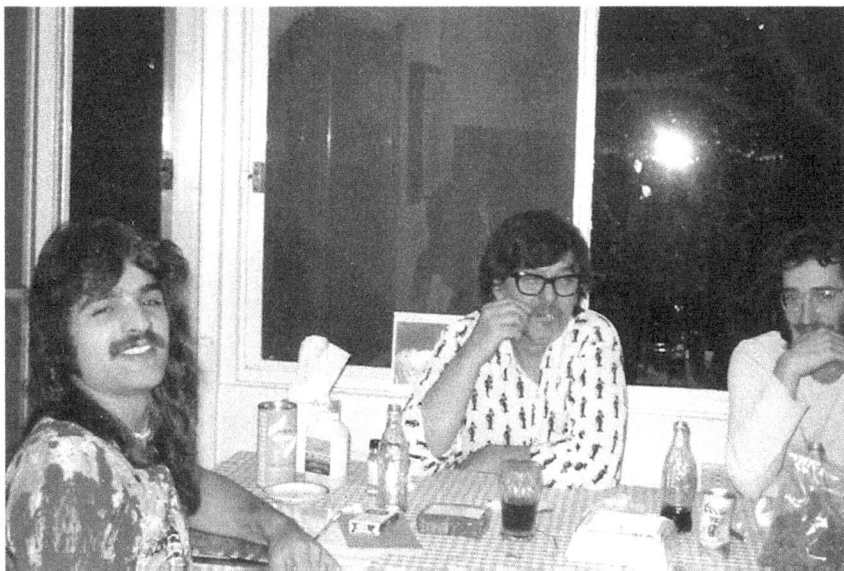

Getting stoned at Dave Hassinger's house with Jeff Cheen on Mulholland Drive in the Hollywood Hills.

Jeanie frosting Frank's hair at the house in Claymont, Delaware.

Frankie toking in the studio.

BANG playing *Harmony Through Music 2* at Ft. Bragg in Fayetteville, North Carolina, on May 24, 1973.

Frankie does glam.

Performing somewhere in the Carolinas.

Poster of BANG show with Lee Pickens Group,
September 1973.

MUSIC album cover.

Wall of cymballs.

MUSIC album photo of the Franks.

CHAPTER 7

The Lost Singles

ON SEPTEMBER 15, 1973, producer Jeff Cheen dropped by in Dallas on some off days to go over the plan to record the singles as opposed to another album. The band played at Concert Mother Earth in Austin, Texas, the next night before flying to Los Angeles to record on the 17th. They began rehearsing on the 18th with Bruce Gary and played the Whiskey A Go Go, with George Clinton's Funkadelic, on September 19th through the 23rd, thanks to Cheen's connections. While playing the Whiskey, on the first day of Autumn, September 21, they recorded "Slow Down," "Feels Nice," and "Make Me Pretty." The next day, they appeared on the *Real Don Steele Show*.

A few minutes before one of the performances at the Whiskey, the new guitarist, Carl Bachman was very quiet and sullen.

"What's wrong?" asked Frank.

"I would rather be in Wilmington, Delaware playing the Sheraton Hotel," replied Bachman.

"The answer blew me away," remembered Frank. "The review of the show summed up what we had become: dazed and confused."

Wrote Dennis Hunt of the *Los Angeles Times*, "The opening act was BANG, a hard rock quartet that, despite some prominent flaws, often verged on excellence. Its performance was awkward, the singing unpolished, and the material infested with an aggravating sameness. But its members are adroit musicians. The set had weak spots but it also included sketches of crackling, volcanic rock and roll music."

A review in the Hollywood Reporter, the next day, said, "Guitarist Carl Bachman's bored look and reluctance to move was a dead weight that detracted from Gilcken's attempt to shake some excitement into the show, which eventually became monotonous."

"Talk about frustration," recalled Frank.

THIS WAS THE same week Gram Parsons, formerly of The Byrds, and Jim Croce died. Parsons overdosed, and Croce perished in a plane crash with five others in Louisiana, while on tour.

ON SEPTEMBER 24TH, after promising Denny that he could play on one song, the band laid down the basic tracks for "Wild Boys." The following week, they worked on overdubs and hung out at the beach. They flew home from Los Angeles on October 2, after firing Denny and Carl.

Said Frank, "The 'lost' singles were recorded at the end of our contract with Capitol. Even though 'Slow Down,' 'Feels Nice,' and 'Make Me Pretty' were great tunes, they died on the vine, getting no support at all from Capitol. Most BANG fans never heard those songs. By then, the writing was on the wall: Capitol had lost interest in us and, in turn, we were very unhappy with their lack of support."

THE BAND ATTEMPTED a return to Los Angeles in November, where they rehearsed with Paul Marshall, the stepson of Larry Gelbart (producer of the television show *M*A*S*H*, etc.) and Bryan Englund, the son of Cloris Leachman, the actress. In early December, while meeting Bryan at his mother's house, she walked out of the bathroom and into the kitchen, naked, with just a towel on her head.

"We were shocked," remembered Frank, "but Bryan acted like it was no big deal."

"Hi!" said the famous Oscar-winning actress, not covering up anything, completely unashamed.

"You gotta love L.A.," said Frank.

DURING THIS TIME, the band's attorney sought settlement from Capitol Records for failing to carry through with the final album. The band was due a $5000 advance, per the contract. Meanwhile, FTF was in touch with Bang Records (no affiliation) about switching labels but nothing came of it.

Just before the end of the year, Frank and Frankie asked for their release and received checks from Capitol Records as settlement for the unrecorded album. They then returned to Philadelphia.

EARLY IN 1974, with the help of their attorney, BANG tried to interest Warner Brothers in their music but nothing came of it. Apparently, no agency or record company was willing to take a chance on a band that had just charted only months before and had been touring the country for over a year with A-listers.

"Unbeknownst to us, we were being black-listed," said Tony. "We could not get a gig. No promoter would hire us. They were told, 'If you hire BANG, you'll never get another act from us.' These guys controlled the whole market."

MEANWHILE, ON JANUARY 24, Muhammad Ali had his re-match with Joe Frazier, promoted as *Super Fight II*. "The King" bested "Smokin' Joe," as he predicted to Tony, by unanimous decision.

THE LAST CAPITOL single, a return to BANG's earlier hard-rocking sound, "Feels Nice" with "Slow Down" (Capitol Records, 3816) was issued by the label on the 16th August, 1974, but the haunting "Make Me Pretty"—with a very similar feel to the *Music* album—never made it to the shops.

"It was never released," confirmed Tony. "A real shame, as it's my favorite BANG song."

...

**"Slow down
Don't run from your dreams
When you know your right
Everybody's waiting
Don't you know somebody needs you tonight**

—Lyrics from *Slow Down*

Whiskey A Go Go ad.

Marquis at the Whiskey A Go Go, September 20, 1973.

Above and below: BANG performing at the Whisky A Go Go.

Frank and Paul Marshall in Hollywood, late 1973.

The Franks with Paul Marshall before the break-up in January 1974.

Assorted show flyers.

CHAPTER 8

Epilogue

"I WAS TALKING on the phone with this guy in California," said Tony. I was talking to him for weeks and when it was time to leave, the whole thing was a sham. It never existed—it was all part of a trick for us to think that we had this whole tour lined up."

"Wow! So, here we are back in Claymont, Delaware, with a new album, three singles, time going by—and we can't work. Nobody will hire us. It finally got to the point, where it was like, 'Hey, it's over.' Incomplete, it ended," lamented Tony.

"We became so frustrated by all the bullshit that we decided to break up the band," said Frank. "Frankie had the opportunity to join a band in Texas. I stayed home working on solo projects, before moving to Texas, then Los Angeles."

BUT, IN THE end, the band was still left with a lot of questions:

What if we had gone with Michael Sunday to Epic Records?

What if Capitol had put a little more behind us?

What if Capitol hadn't had the management changes?

What if we hadn't fallen out with Rick Bowen?

What if Tony hadn't been fired as the drummer?

What if Herb Belkin had taken us to Atlantic?

THE FRANKS MOVED back east in the mid-1980s and reformed BANG in 1999. A new album, *Return To Zero*, was recorded and released at the end of that year, with the more metal-oriented

The Maze (featuring new versions of old favorites "Love Sonnet" and "Bow To The King") following, in 2004.

"The three of us realized that BANG was still a musical force," said Frank Ferrara, "and even though a lot of years had passed, we were writing songs as if it were yesterday. The dream is alive and with a renewed thirst and love of the music, we are resuming our quest."

The band's *BANG* album was recently added to *Decibel Magazine*'s Decibel Hall of Fame, containing the greatest heavy metal records of all time. After several decades and despite the band being buried by the label and the promoter, BANG's creation with producer Michael Sunday—the album written in only ten days to sound like Sabbath, Zeppelin, and Grand Funk—had finally taken its rightful place in rock and roll history.

Says Frank, "Remember, you don't stop playing because you get old, you get old because you stop playing. The magic is still alive."

Frank Ferrara and Frankie Gilcken from the original lineup reformed BANG in 2014. They started touring again and have since done two European tours to the delight of enthusiastic fans. The quest continues . . .

For more information or to keep up with BANG, please see the website at: www.bangmusic.com

...

**"Must you be a superstar
To find your means of living
Does it matter who you are
Can't you stomach giving**

—Lyrics from *Questions*

BANG Delaware license plate.

BANG moms.

BANG 8-track tape.

Rick and Donna Bowen.

Frank Ferrara.

Frankie Gilcken.

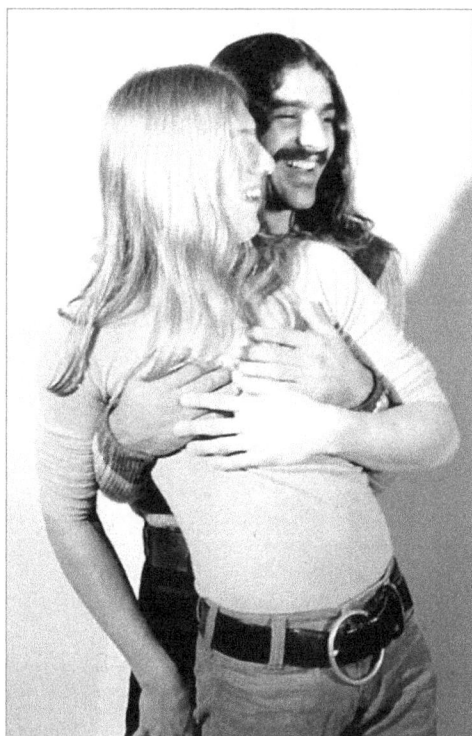

The Franks goofing off at a photo shoot.

BANGgirl (artist: Danny Simmonds).

BANG in Concert poster (artist: Danny Simmonds).

Tracks

Death of a Country

Death of a Country
No Trespassing
My Window
Life On Ending
Certainly Meaningless
Future Song

BANG

Lions, Christians
The Queen
Last Will And Testament
Our Home
Future Shock
Questions
Come with Me
Redman

Mother/Bow to the King

Mother
Humble
Keep On
Idealist...Realist
Feel the Hurt
Tomorrow
Bow to the King

Music

Windfair
Glad Your Home
Don't Need Nobody
Page of my Life
Love Sonnet
Must Be Love
Exactly Who I Am
Pearl and Her Ladies
Little Boy Blue
Brightness
Another Town

Lost Singles

Slow Down
Feels Nice
Make Me Pretty

LPs

Title (Format)	Label	Cat#	Country	Year
Bang (LP, Album)	Capitol Records	ST-11015	US	1972
Bang (8-Trk, Album)	Capitol Records	8XT-11015	US	1972
Bang (Cass, Album)	Capitol Records	4XT-11015	US	1972
Bang (LP, Album)	Capitol Records	EST-11015	UK	1972
Bang (LP, Album)	Capitol Records	3C 062-81148	Italy	1972
Bang (LP, Album)	Capitol Records	ST-11015	Canada	1972
Bang (LP, Album)	Capitol Records	SLEM-364	Mexico	1972
Bang (LP, Album)	Capitol Records	ECP-80559	Japan	1972
Bang (LP, Album)	Capitol Records	ST-11015	US	1972
Bang (LP, Album, MP)	Capitol Records	ST-11-15	US	1972
Bang (CD, Album)	Lizard Records (9)	LR0707-2	Germany	1998
Bang (LP, Album, Pic, Ltd, Num, RE)	Outlaw Recordings	OLR-014	US	2002
Bang (LP, Album, Pic, RE, Ltd, MP)	Outlaw Recordings	OLR-014	US	2002
Bang (LP, Album, RE)	Green Tea Records	GTR 133-1	Germany	2010
Bang (CD, dig)	Svart Records	SVR397CD	Finland	2016
Bang (LP, Album, RE, Cle)	Svart Records	SVR397	Finland	2016
Bang (LP, Album, RE, Gat)	Svart Records	SVR397	Finland	2016
Mother / Bow To The King (LP, Gat)	Capitol Records	SMAS-11110	US	1972
Mother/Bow To The King (LP, Album)	Capitol Records	ECP-80680	Japan	1972
Mother/Bow To The King (LP, Album)	Capitol Records	1 C 062-81 329	Germany	1972
Mother/Bow To The King (CD, Album, RE)	Lizard Records (4)	LR 0709-2	Germany	1999
Mother / Bow To The King (LP, Gat)	Green Tea Records	GTR-134-1	Germany	2010
Mother / Bow To The King (CD, dig)	Svart Records	SVR451CD	Finland	2016
Mother / Bow To The King (LP, Album, RE)	Svart Records	SVR451	Finland	2016
Mother / Bow To The King (LP, Album, RE, Ora)	Svart Records	SVR451	Finland	2016
Music (LP, Album)	Capitol Records	ST-11190	US	1973
Music (8-Trk, Album)	Capitol Records	8XT-11190	US	1973
Music (CD, vin)	Rise Above	ra 040	UK & Euope	2005
Music (LP, Album, RE, RM)	Green Tea Records	GTR-138-1	Europe	2011
Music & Lost Singles (CD, dig)	Svart Records	SVR454CD	Finland	2016
Music (LP, Album, RE, RM + 7", EP)	Svart Records	SVR454	Finland	2016
Music (LP, Album, RE, RM, Red + 7", EP, Red)	Svart Records	SVR454	Finland	2016
Death Of A Country (LP, Bla)	Rise Above Relics	RARLP015	UK	2011
Death Of A Country (LP, Cle)	Rise Above Relics	RARLP015	UK	2011

Title (Format)	Label	Cat#	Country	Year
Death Of A Country (LP, Pur)	Rise Above Relics	RARLP015	UK	2011
Death Of A Country (LP, Yel)	Rise Above Relics	RARLP015	UK	2011
Death Of A Country (CD, Album, RE)	Svart Records	SVR455CD	Finland	2016
Death Of A Country (LP, Album, Ltd, RE)	Svart Records	SVR455	Finland	2016
Death Of A Country (LP, Ltd, RE, Blu)	Svart Records	SVR455	Finland	2016

SINGLES

Title (Format)	Label	Cat#	Country	Year
Questions / Future Shock (7", Single)	Capitol Records	3304	US	1972
Questions / Future Shock (7", Single)	Capitol Records	ECR-10075	Japan	1972
Questions / Future Shock (7", Single)	Capitol Records	3304	Canada	1972
Questions / Future Shock (7", Single)	Capitol Records	1 C 006-81 116	Germany	1972
Questions / Future Shock (7", Single, Yel)	Capitol Records	5C 006-81 116	Germany	1972
Questions (7")	Capitol Records	CL 15722	UK	1972
Questions (7")	Capitol Records	2C-006-81116	France	1972
Questions (7", Promo)	Capitol Records	CL 15722	UK	1972
Questions (7", Single, Mono, Promo)	Capitol Records	PRO-6465, P-3304	US	1972
No Sugar Tonight / Idealist Realist (7", Single)	Capitol Records	3474	US	1972
No Sugar Tonight (7", Single, Mono, Promo)	Capitol Records	P-3474	US	1972
No Sugar Tonight / Idealist Realist (7", Single)	Movieplay	SN - 20.748	Spain	1972
No Sugar Tonight / Idealist Realist (7", Single)	Capitol Records	ECR-10227	Japan	1972
No Sugar Tonight / Idealist Realist (7", Single)	Capitol Records	2C 006-81339	France	1972
No Sugar Tonight / Idealist Realist (7", Single)	Capitol Records	3474	Canada	1972
Keep On / Redman (7", Single)	Capitol Records	3386	US	1972
Keep On / Redman (7", Single)	Capitol Records	1 J –6-81.228	Spain	1972
Keep On (7", Single)	Capitol Records	681228	France	1972
Keep On (7", Single, Mono, Promo)	Capitol Records	PRO-6657, P-3386	US	1972
Redman / Keep On (7", Single)	Capitol Records	S 45-78770	Brazil	1972
Must Be Love / Love Sonnet (7", Single)	Capitol Records	3622	US	1973
Must Be Love (7", Single, Promo)	Capitol Records	P-3622	US	1973
Feels Nice / Slow Down (7", Single)	Capitol Records	3816	US	1974
Feels Nice (7", Single, Promo)	Capitol Records	P-3816	US	1974

Lyrics

Death of a Country

Living isn't as good as it seems
Our country's dying before our eyes
What has happened to cause this scene
They say we're trying but it's only lies

The man put us here to do good things
Things to make him proud
To keep us down he gave no wings
To tell our fears we must be loud

Our countries dying its breathing choked
It's blood is filled with sin
And of its skin it's pocked with sores
Where cold clean flesh had been

Can you hear the sounds of progress
Landing on the moon
Can you hear the sounds of violence
Banging at your door
Can you hear the sounds of laughter
Coming from the streets

Looks like nothing is the same
People turning me around
I don't even know my name
Gettin' tired of this cold world
It's enough to bring you down

[*continued on next page*]

[Death of a Country *continued*]

Lies
Gettin' tired of the same same lies
Lies
All those lies
Can't take my eyes from all those lies

Can you hear the sounds of progress
Landing on the moon
Can you hear the sounds of violence
Banging on your door
Can you hear the sounds of laughter
Coming from the streets

Understand what this song's about
It's a warning for you and me
Look around when you go outside
You'll feel...you'll smell...you'll see

We gotta do something it won't be long
Come on and lend a hand
Give back what was given to us
Natures legacy a healthy man

No Trespassing

Flowers dotting unlit worlds
Men are searching lustered pearls

Reaching far and grasping quick
Men set out within their ship

Future's gone it's present now
Stars abound to show us how
Find the answer to our dream
Knowing it we'll want to scream

Turn us back we shouldn't go
Our way is blocked our hope is low
Shining thru the beaded glass
We watch the years begin to pass

Backwards further time goes by
From blue to red we watch the sky
Land in masses then steaming earth
Further back to watch the birth

Days are gone it's always night
The sun is blocked from our sight
Giant mountains of harden mud
Pouring out earth's molten blood

Further back 'til all's at ease
A giant hand comes like a breeze
It signals peace it gives us fear
God pulls our plug we're stranded here

My Window

It shows its scene without a choice
It's looking eye is but a voice
Reflecting sights that cause a time
When helpless man begins to find

The changing force of sinful ways
The chilling thoughts of lonely days
Now I sit with shaven hair
My body's strapped I fear this chair

All right now

Fate's a yell in times ever now
One lives his life in quest of hope
Seeing speaking tells a tale
Of how to live to each his own

I scream but ears have lost my sound
I cannot breathe I'm gagged and bound
A crime of hate I have to bear
A fear of death this electric chair

The twisting winds of death unfold
My body slumps I'm damp and cold
Place my mind with nurtured needs
Upon the lawn of fertile seeds

Let me speak with lips sewn shut
Of things I've done in mortal state

Fate's a yell in times ever now
One lives his life in quest of hope
Seeing speaking tells a tale
Of how to live to each his own

I cannot scream so no one hears me
They dare not look they show their fears
My window's there the scene's the same
I'm not here they've lost my name

Life on Ending

For countless hours I think of life
My being seems meant to be
My thoughts are bright my mind is clear
My body shakes with health and fear

Morning's gone the time stands still
I look at life it brings a chill
Before you came I was not known
Now you leave I'm still alone

I see a future burning near
I'm not included you left me here
Time has gone it's closed its eye
My God I'm scared don't let me die

I know that you don't wanna see me
Walking on your velvet floor
Why don't you even wanna hear me
Knocking at your golden door

Well there's something I must tell you
Before I go before I go yeah
I've got to leave this place
Gotta see you Lord

Gotta see my Lord ... gotta see you Lord
Gotta see my Lord ... gotta see you Lord
Gotta see my Lord

I see a future burning near
I'm not included you left me here
Time has gone it's closed its eye
My God I'm scared don't let me die ... die

Certainly Meaningless

Greeting Gods of marbled stone
Seizing nature on its terms
Tunneled love comes caving in
Deserting us to where we've been

Statues melt from molten lies
Bits of sand infect my eyes
Pull your head from putrid cheese
Rape your mouth with stilling breeze

Keep abreast of turmoiled times
Prudent people mouth their lines
Watch them work at being not
Pump their ears make them hot

Mellow melons rot with age
So does man within a cage
Unknown orphans reach their peak

Greeting Gods of marbled stone

Future Song

Flowing softly pinkish foam
Clinging mass of swirling waste
Eyes behold a sight of gloom
Churning flesh come sliding home

Bees and Birds their wings grown old
Their speed has gone their legs deformed

Tiny thoughts that never grew
Are lost among the wetless dew

Smoking rafts are floating high
Reveal the deeds of days gone by

Earth's own shroud now looks of gray
Its seas and trees have turned to hay

Echoes greet the ones who yell
Warring tribes now own the world
Science learning a search for truth
Have slid beneath the roaming puke

Man was great he touched the stars
Now he breeds in rusty cars
Where once stood cities spiraling high

Now hangs death a poisoned sky

Lions, Christians

Shaking hiding from their sight
We dread to feel their angered might
We cannot run from this fate
Unjust rewards they make us wait

We all denied their pagan ways
We must suffer their deadly sport
It might take hours and it might take days
Our time on earth is growing short

No more pain and wondering why
We're with our God he heard our cry
We had the vision and now we are free
Our screams will live in history

We're herded to the bloodstained ground
They tell us death by starving hounds
Our skin our bones they'll desecrate
Our souls our faith they'll never take

Our lot was drawn we chose our Lord
We knew we'd die by beast or sword
Our fear of God was strong stronger than
Our fear of death our fear of man

No more pain and wondering why
We're with our God he heard our cry
We had the vision and now we are free
Our screams will live in history

The Queen

Yesterday she ran her house
Milking bashful buyers
When money creased her waiting hand
She catered strange desires

Her splendid easy woman
Would gladly grace your side
Beneath their creamy ecstasy
Revealing scars they hide

Beneath the glow of a neon sky
She vowed to find her fame
No matter what the price may be
She'd do it just the same
No matter what the price may be
She'd do it just the same

Then one day a mark appeared
Set for any price
Requesting service so bizarre
No one could he entice

The Queen alone could see delight
In his twisted head
With racing pulse and burning thighs
She led him to her bed

Beneath the glow of a neon sky
She vowed to find her fame
No matter what the price may be
She'd do it just the same
And now we watch her closing door
Her joy will soon take wing
Her need for fame is over now
The Queen has found a king

Last Will and Testament

A year has passed it's deadly course
Your friends and family sit with remorse
It's time to read what's left to them
Of all the wealth you couldn't spend

Your lawyer's filled with wit and greed
Begin at once your will to read
Sneaky smiles they cross their mouths

Happy people make their way
Through the world everyday
Saddened people they can't seem to find
Their way across that rejected line
I'm pushed along by uncaring hordes
They're always crawling moving towards
That pot of gold up in the sky
The one that seems to pass them by

If death should forestall my life
My worldly goods I leave my wife
She's undeserving was just a private whore
Yet she never locked her bedroom door
In times of need she was always there
My tears my pain she'd always share

Forgetting memories of our past
They want their splendid life to last
They start with love avoiding hate
Let each one earn their ending fate
Let each one earn their ending fate

Come with Me

Everyone come with me
Leave your world come and see
Do the things you like to do
Come with me for eternity

No pain can't go insane
No work can't go berserk
Just happy days no worldly ways
Never eat never sleep
Yeah

Explore a path of peaceful dreams
Forget those dreary bummer scenes
No evil eye no need to lie
In simple ways we'll live our days

No pain can't go insane
No work can't go berserk
Just happy days no worldly ways
Never eat never sleep
Yeah

Your friends are gone it won't be long
Leave your world come with me
Your friends are gone it won't be long
Leave your world come with me

Everyone come with me
Leave your world come and see
Do the things you like to do
Come with me for eternity

No pain can't go insane
No work can't go berserk
Just happy days no worldly ways
Never eat never sleep
Yeah

Our Home

White sand majestic sparkling snow
Clean rivers unspoiled free to flow
He gave these treasures for our home
Uncaring destruction we have shown

Our gift we've wasted it yeah
We've thrown away yeah
This was to be our home

This was to be our home
This was to be our home
This was to be our home
Yeah

Starving victims fleeing blindly
Fighting death's clutching hand
Tin foiled hot dogs by the thousands
Rotting sweetly on the land

Unread leaflets bless your doorstep
Reeking rivers filled with foam
Sulfur clouds gag each new day
My God this was to be our home

This was to be our home
This was to be our home
This was to be our home
Yeah Our Home
Yeah Our Home

Future Shock

Can you feel those tidal waves
Slashing knifes of endless change
Screwing up your patterned lives
Raining down wretched strife

Hashish dreams
Junkie schemes
Crocodile tears
Escape your fears

Apathetic nine to five
Cashing paychecks to survive
Vandals lurking in the streets
Gloat behind their worthless feats

Hashish dreams
Junkie schemes
Crocodile tears
Escape your fears

Crying
Dying
Future Shock

Teenyboppers idolize
Cash and carry packaged highs
Figurines stalk your space
Home is nothing but a place

Fearing ours will be there fate
Those across the water wait
Creeping tides mount their shore
Ominous rumble groans to roar

Hashish dreams
Junkie schemes
Crocodile tears
Escape your fears

Crying
Dying
Future Shock

Questions

Have you ever felt the night
Felt the wind around you
Have you read a book or two
Or have books been reading you

Do clothes affect your mental health
Are your boots reheeled
Could you lead a life of wealth
Delivered wrapped and sealed

Questions all around me
Questions bring me down
Questions all around me
Questions bring me down

Must you be a superstar
To find your means of living
Does it matter who you are
Can't you stomach giving

Questions all around me
Questions bring me down
Questions all around me
Questions bring me down

Redman

Nations died and lost their land
Sacred ground turned to sand
Our leaders words the cries of their kin
Swirl around us adrift in the wind

A weapon of war invaded mankind
Fatal germs killed all left behind
Sparing those few who fled under ground
Unlike the Redman would never be found

We all need a wishing star
A spirit to tell us who we are
Our future's unclear it's baked in the clay
Give us the chance to start a new day
Start a new day

Why we were spared we may never know
We're given a choice a gun or a bow
Beneath our feet the survivors have died
Again through the calm of nature we ride

We all need a wishing star
A spirit to tell us who we are
Our future's unclear its baked in the clay
We have the chance to start a new day
Start a new day

Mother

Mother ... You've been good to me
Mother ... Kept me from what I shouldn't see
Taught me life was sweet and grand
Told me goodness came from man
Mother ... you lied to me
Oh you ... you lied to me

All those years in your arms
Tucked away from worldly harms
Behind you apron strings I saw
Life was happy free to all

Mother ... take a look around
Mother ... take a look at what I found
Greedy people everywhere
No compassion they just don't care
Mother ... you lied to me
Oh you ... you lied to me

All those years in your arms
Tucked away from worldly harms
Behind your apron strings I saw
Life was happy free to all

Mother ... why was I conceived
Given life then made to breathe
Born through love then tossed away
Left to face the world each day
Mother ... you lied to me
Oh you ... you lied to me

Humble

We need to know our destined fate
We need to know don't make us wait
Tell me the answers tell me now
Give me direction show me how

Let me know what's planned for me
Pain and sorrow won't let me be
Can you tell me won't you share
Your mystic secrets don't you care

You have the power
You have the might
To change the world from wrong to right
Why make us suffer live alone
Let us live in your worldly home

Through countless times you ruled all things
Gave life to man created kings
Were we made to touch his lips
Then kneel in fear humbleness

Keep On

Keep on the door will close
Close and lock you away
Cold winds wait the sun don't shine
Look at all you leave behind

Keep on the door will close
Close and lock you in
Steal your loneliness
Take you where you've never been

Keep on the path is clear
See the truth it's coming near
Lose yourself behind the door
No one wants you anymore

Keep on the door will close
Close and lock you away
Cold winds wait the sun don't shine
Look at all you leave behind

Keep on the door will close
Close and lock you out
Icy fingers wait to shake your hand
Take your life if they can

Keep on the door will close
Close and lock you away
Cold winds wait the sun don't shine
Look at all you leave behind

Idealist...Realist

Hey look at me I'm just like you
Abused through out the day
No matter what we do or say
We hurt someone something some way

When will you see the light
When will you start your change
You need not suffer
Just find a way to rearrange

Idealists dream of flowered worlds
The realist feels the dirt
No matter what we try to seek
It will not come and kiss our cheek

No time to taste your mother's pie
Or freak the ones you meet
Don't let your life just wonder by
Make it something clean and sweet

Feel The Hurt

Should I think about my sorrow
That I know I can not change
So distant seems my happiness
So real is my pain

You gave me a reason to live
But now you've gone away
I need someone to help me
Make it through the day

I've searched through many teardrops
I feel I can't go on
My burden seems so heavy
Each hour seems so long

So distant seems my happiness
So real is my pain
I feel I'm losing the one I love
I feel I'm losing you

Should I think about my sorrow
That I know I can not change
So distant seems my happiness
So real is my pain

You gave me a reason to live
But now you've gone away
I need someone to help me
Make it through the day

Tomorrow

So today you're not happy
Happy at all
Why don't you tell me
Tell me it all
Don't turn your face don't make me guess
Tell me I'll listen
The hurt will be less
The hurt will be less

Tomorrow may be a beautiful day
Tomorrow may bring a much better way
To find your place and what you must do
To face all the problems that are facing you

You need a friend a listening ear
Someone to talk to
Someone sincere
Knowing arms to hold you tight
Someone to be with
Thru out the night
Thru out the night

Tomorrow may be a beautiful day
Tomorrow may bring a much better way
To find your place and what you must do
To face all the problems that are facing you
That are facing you
That are facing you

Bow to the King

Bow to the King
He's marching down the aisle
His subjects start to scream
They've waited quite a while

The King is dressed in red
His fists are hard as lead
He's waited months to meet
The man he's going to beat
Bow to the King

He slowly steps inside
Across the canvas hide
He hears the bell to fight
He's blinded by the light
Bow to the King

The King begins to move
His movements are so smooth
The man moves to his right
His eyes are filled with fright

The King connects a right
The man is turning white
A jab has crushed his jaw
The man begins to fall

In fifteen seconds flat
He's put him on the mat
The man is counted out
The King has won the bout

As the bell begins to ring
The crowd salutes their king
With fists up high they jab the sky
He's won again they sing

Windfair

I'm finally approaching
The end of a dream
Although I'm to perish
It's not what it seems
The Windfair's gliding
It's locked to it's course
My circus like ending
Will bring no remorse

The task that's before me
Is stated quite clear
Destroy the intruders
They shouldn't be here
Just laying the problem
Before me sincere
Was all that I needed
Needed to hear

I'm tracing a vision I chose
Please take my crying for it's joy that it shows
So give me my orders and let me get there
I've waited so long such a lifetime
To guide the Windfair

She's not much to look at
Her dents and her rust
She was my father's
A ship you could trust
Oh man did he love her
No wrong could she do
And I know yes I know
I'm loving her too

I'm tracing a vision I chose
Please take my crying for it's joy that it shows
So give me my orders and let me get there
I've waited so long such a lifetime
To guide the Windfair

Glad Your Home (For returning POW's)

So now your home and it's not the same
Every things different things have changed
The TV will bore you that tube's been a waste
You've seen destruction watched death face to face
The Beatles have gone they've gone their own way
Music's transformed it's got much more to say

How can we tell you all the changes you've missed
The way we've been acting the asses we've kissed
You missed being hip and the phrases we'd chat
Like "doing my thing" and "that's where it's at"

We're sorry you've suffered
You feel you've been had
You've missed quite a lot
Some good mostly bad
We've been to the moon
Felt its dust in our hands
But what's that to you
If you can't understand

You missed all the flares the bell bottom blues
Hair is the fashion you feel you've been used
Don't get me wrong I'm sorry for you
For what you must face I just couldn't go through

So try and understand what's come and gone by
It's been for the best so stop wondering why
And let me say this before it's all shown
Welcome home man we're glad that your home
We're glad your home
We're so glad
Glad your home

Don't Need Nobody

Pushed around up and down
We started to lose our way
Wanting one thing
Then made to do another
Oh Lord there's gotta be a better way

We don't need nobody to tell us what we want
Cause now we know yes we know
We don't need nobody to tell us what we want
Cause now we know yes we know

Miles and miles
Always on the go
We played to all the waiting ears
Did our trip the best way we knew how
And conquered all our fears

We don't need nobody to tell us what we want
Cause now we know yes we know
We don't need nobody to tell us what we want
Cause now we know yes we know

People thought we were too young to know our minds
Thought they knew
Think they know
But now we'll show them in the best way we know how
So here we go
Here we go

Page of my Life

Look in my diary the book of my life
Each page that is written tells of the strife
The memories of living long lonely years
Stained with a hundred a thousand dried tears

Every page echoes a world that was mine
A world full of hardships a world so unkind
Each page a story reflecting my past
All of the people we're parts of the cast

The good ones I met
The ones that I despised
All the hurts
All the lies

Yet one page is clear no pen bears its mark
That time of my life apart from the dark
When you came to me so fresh and so new
That one page I'll save to remind me of you

But now you're gone I'm lonely again
Your name will be written I'm holding the pen
To write how you left never saying goodbye
To close out this chapter I'm still wondering why

The good ones I met
The ones that I despised
All the hurts
All the lies

Love Sonnet

Time honored dreams can be reality
Changing to now what was before
Love is ever at its height
Love is yes when its right

When one loves his life is still
His dreams and wishes all come true

Beneath the stars of scented skies
My arms reach out to hold
The warmth of love with all its sighs
A love that I must hold

Love can be a mounting sound
Expanding till hearts grow full
Love can be a friendship found
Love can turn the fire cool

Time honored dreams can be reality
Changing to now what was before
Love is ever at its height
Love is Yes
When its right

Must Be Love

What makes you happy
What make you sad
What makes the day bright
What makes you glad
What makes you want to scream out loud
What makes you reach up for the clouds

It must be love
It must be love

What gives you good times
What makes you live from day to day
What keeps you hanging on
When you can't have your way
What makes you feel so free
What brings you close to me

It must be love
It must be love
It must be love
It must be love

What wakes you every morning
Puts you to sleep at night
Gives you smiles in the daytime
Makes you feel so right

It must be love
It must be love

Exactly Who I Am

My life's been full of sorrow
I've tried to tell myself maybe tomorrow
Most all the things in life I ever cared about
It seems I could not have

I've wasted years of precious time
I spent my life trying to find
A way to prove
A way to boast
To all the world
Myself the most

Exactly Who and what I think I am

I've lived a life of shattered dreams
Been cool and held inside my screams
Now I sit and wonder
Why and where my biggest dream has gone

I've wasted years of precious time
I spent my life trying to find
A way to prove
A way to boast
To all the world
Myself the most

Exactly Who and what I think I am

Pearl and Her Ladies

Amazing colossal fantastic reviews
Pearl and her ladies were making big news
Since they hit town with banners and signs
The theater on main street has long waiting lines

Down through the streets strutting with class
Thirteen musicians led Pearl to her task
To perform for the people their wildest dreams
An erotic adventure with live sexual scenes

A preacher a rabbi a priest and a nun
Banning together to stop all the fun
Pearl and her ladies with tattoos on their arms
Dressed in there finest revealing their charms

They met at the corner of Lincoln and Bell
Tension was heavy in the air was the smell
Of perfume and whiskey where ever you stood
To witness the showdown of evil and good

The rest of the story is hazy and dim
Years gone by since Pearl sold her sin
The last thing I heard she died of old age
Going out with a BANG
And three men on a stage
Going out with a BANG
And three men on a stage

Little Boy Blue

Oh Little Boy Blue
Now where you going to
Your eyes are showing tears
I've never seen before
Sure it's hard but you'll get by
For someday soon
Your gonna find
What you've been waiting for

Look beyond the stars
To your dreams that shine forever on
Look past the shadows
For they'll remain until your dead and gone
Don't you know
Everything will work out in the end my friend

Oh Little Boy Blue
Don't be sad it's true
That all your dreams will turn the dark back into day
Can't you see there's always hope
There's no one there who can take it all away

Look beyond the stars
To your dreams that shine forever on
Look past the shadows
For they'll remain until your dead and gone
Don't you know
Everything will work out in the end my friend

Oh Little Boy Blue
Now where you going to
Your eyes are showing tears
I've never seen before
Showing tears I've never seen before

Brightness

There were times when we sang
Many times when we laughed
But I remember when we looked
And saw brightness in each others eyes
We saw brightness in each others eyes

Happy hours spent knowing who we were
Apart from the busy scenes around us
When we touched not to explore
Rather to feel our love together
Rather to feel our love together

Teach Me
I wanna learn
Love Me
I want to dream
Touch Me
I wanna feel
Hear Me
I wanna know

Now I wait for love to bring
A song of love that I can sing
A song to tell the world of you
And all the plans that we plan to do
All the plans that we plan to do
We saw brightness in each others eyes
We saw brightness in each others eyes

Another Town (instrumental)

Slow Down

Slow down
Touch your life
Don't you know there's friends to be found
Lift your eyes and see the world
Lift your eyes up from the ground

Slow down
Don't run from your dreams
When you know they're right
Everybody's waiting
Don't you know somebody needs you tonight

Slow down
Find love and be wise
Slow down
Dry the tears from your eyes
Slow down
Find yourself once again
Slow down
Slow down my friend

Slow down
Don't run from your dreams
When you know they're right
Everybody's waiting
Don't you know somebody needs you tonight

Slow down
Find love and be wise
Slow down
Dry the tears from your eyes
Slow down
Find yourself once again
Slow down
Slow down my friend

Feels Nice

Wait let me through there's so much I gotta do
Gotta get down the road to you and love you
Oh how good it feels to know
We're gonna take it all so slow
Gonna hold on never let you go and love you

do do do do do do do
do do do do do do do

Your just a loving woman
Trying to get it on with me
You can make me feel so good
I ain't never gonna let you be
I'm just a loving man
Trying to get it on with you
I can make you feel so good
Look out I'm coming too

Aw feels nice
I can't remember anything so good
Aw feels nice
I love to squeeze
I wonder if I should

do do do do do do do
do do do do do do do

Make Me Pretty

Please Mister cameraman
Take my picture if you can
Shoot me good
She wants to see
Make me pretty

Her letter had a shot of her
She sent her love to me "Dear Sir"
See her eyes
Is it love that glows within
Have I found that special someone
She loves a name
Am I him

You see I'm here and she's out there
We never met face to face
I can't get out she can't come in
Have I found that special someone
She loves a name
Am I him

We met by pen six months ago
I had no friends no place to go
She read my ad in "Lonely Friends"
The magazine my mother always sends to me

Make me pretty make me sweet
Make me someone she loves to see
Can I be the one she sees
Can I answer all her needs

Should I tell her where I've been
Is it love that glows within
Have I found that special someone
She loves a name
Am I him
She loves a name
Am I him

Acknowledgments

CAPITOL RECORDS: Herb Belkin

OUR PRODUCERS: Michael Sunday
Jeff Cheen
Ron & Howie Albert

OUR ENGINEERS: Karl Richardson
Dave Hassinger

OUR MUSIC PUBLISHERS: Victor Benedetto
Jimmy Ienner

OUR BANDMATES: Duris Maxwell
Gary Osier
Mace Maben
Bob Johnson
Denny D'Agostino
Carl Bachman
Paul Marshall

ADDITIONAL MUSICANS & CREW: Joe Hooker
George Emmertz
Dennis Westman
Tim Trainor

EARLY MANAGERS: Paul Lichter
Jay Felkoff

PHOTOGRAPHY: Carl Dunn
and to the many others that
we never knew

SUNBURY PRESS: Lawrence Knorr
Crystal Devine

THANK YOU EVERYONE!!!

- IN MEMORIUM -

Karen Young	Jan. 6, 1991
Herb Belkin	Aug. 22, 2001
George Emmertz	Dec. 31, 2001
Steve Hiner	Mar. 21, 2005
Bruce Gary	Aug. 22, 2006
Dave Hassinger	Aug. 15, 2007
Mace Maben	Mar. 21, 2012
John Palladino	Dec. 20, 2015
Muhammad Ali	June 3, 2016

References

Interview with Tony Diorio September 26, 2014.

Interview with Frank Ferrara November 26, 2014.

Interview with Frank Ferrara & Tony Diorio December 10, 2014.

Interview of Tommy Wingate February 16, 2015.

Interview of Michael Sunday February 18, 2015.

Interview of Rick Bowan February 19, 2015.

Interview of Karl Richardson February 23, 2015.

Interview of Jeff Cheen February 25, 2015.

Interview of Donna Bowan, Tommy Wingate, and Danny Simmonds March 4, 2015.

Interview with Frankie Gilcken December 20, 2015.

Numerous newspaper accounts from Newspapers.com.

Album and singles information from discogs.com.

Index

Lightning Source UK Ltd.
Milton Keynes UK
UKHW011359121118
332201UK00001B/269/P